THE POINT AND FIGURE METHOD
OF
ANTICIPATING STOCK PRICE MOVEMENTS

Complete Theory and Practice

By

VICTOR de VILLIERS

Author of

"Financial Independence at Fifty" (Magazine of Wall St.)
"Building and Holding Your Fortune" (The Financial World)
"How to Buy Low and Sell High" (Ticker Publishing Co.)
"Detecting Buying and Selling Points in Securities"
(Magazine of Wall St.)

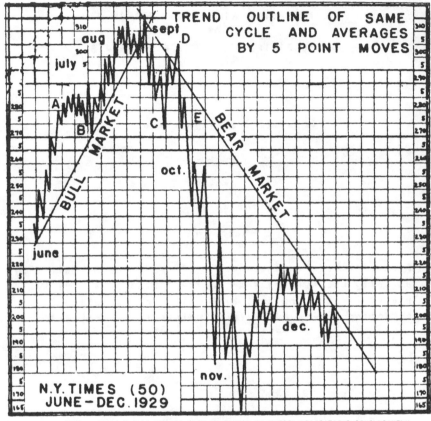

TREND   OUTLINE   OF   SAME
CYCLE   AND   AVERAGES
BY   5   POINT   MOVES

BULL MARKET

BEAR MARKET

N.Y. TIMES (50)
JUNE–DEC. 1929

THE INVESTOR AND LONG PULL TRADER MUST BE GUIDED BY THESE IMPLICATIONS CONCLUSIVELY

A.   Area of caution; either consolidation of gain, resistance, or distribution.
B.   16 point major reaction; about half way in main trend; shows inside support.
C.   Perfect double bottom. Carry nothing below this area again!
D.   Practical but perfect double top; but below main trend line. This was the best sell-
     ing signal of the entire cycle -- in conjunction with C.
E.   Secondary critical zone of inside support. If this is abandoned proof conclusive
     that -- cycle completed.
$$$. Place for stops, for investors or traders. It was inexcusable to carry stocks below
     $$$.

PUBLISHERS' PREFACE

This masterpiece on Point & Figure by Victor deVilliers is an accepted classic of market literature. This printing is an exact duplication of the original 1933 edition.

Windsor Books
Brightwaters, N.Y. 11718

6

The Point and Figure Method is complete in itself. If no other data or guide to market price movements were available, or if the selection of a *single plan* as the basis of anticipating stock price movements became imperative to the exclusion of all others, I would earnestly recommend the serious consideration of this *inside* Method as most reliable.

Accept then, this well-tried and proven guide and Method, with the author's endorsement of its practical value. It is a substantial segment of the sum and substance of tested practices in price path appraisement. It is highly valued by men, organizations, institutions and interests who know its worth.

Victor de Villiers

New York, N. Y.
June 1933.

---

* "You must clear away the debris of the 1929 crash of false principles and learn to use a mass of new-found knowledge and development, in such a way as to make it the servant rather than the lunatic master of mankind." Bernard M. Baruch, former Chairman of the War Industries Board, in a speech at annual commencement exercises of Oglethorpe University. (Author's note:- The Point and Figure Method rests on a scientific basis, it is old and proven. It may prove to be "new found knowledge" to many. --V de V.)

THE POINT AND FIGURE METHOD

OF ANTICIPATING STOCK PRICE MOVEMENTS

I. THE WEIGHT OF AUTHORITY BEHIND

THIS METHOD

This Method has grown from crude beginnings more than fifty years ago, receiving limited, private and rather cautious recognition at about the commencement of the present century. It has been intimated that this Method was used during the time of the U. S. Steel merger (1901) by Mr. James R. Keene in charge of the Steel Pool. He was a skilled tape reader and market student. This shrewd observer and a close coterie of his friends were said to have been initiated into some of its secrets and their practical applications.

Historical discussion serves no useful purpose. Like Topsy, the Method has probably "growed," and developed with improvements and re-finements. In our time, in the course of studying, imparting, and in-stalling the data for the benefit of investment interests (bankers, capitalists and operators), we have simplified, refined and improved both the data and Method. Substantially, the present Method, its data and the results found of greatest benefit, are here recorded for your consideration in this work.

Confidence may be had in the ultimate efficacy of the Point and Figure Method, and its superiority in many respects over others. This is because of the reliance placed upon it by important financial inter-ests, substantial operators and capitalists, having significant commit-ments depending on its findings, and bankers using it as a background for their decisions. Many organizations having the supervision of millions of dollars, financial counselors whose success depends upon consistent accuracy, and market advisory institutions upon whose aver-age success their permanent welfare depends, rely upon it. May we add in all modesty, that the Point and Figure Method in its original ramifica-tions as learned by us and subsequently improved, has proven a "sheet anchor to the windward" in many a storm?

The data to be kept and preserved will be described in detail. There is weighty authority behind this *data*, and the necessity for re-specting its requirements. We found by the trial and error method what became essential and more important what could be dispensed with. It was discovered that it was impossible to overestimate the importance of checking and rechecking conclusions by this Method, and by other tests, some of which this author has devised and used satisfactorily for many years. They are herewith described for the first time.

This Method, devoid of mystery and complication, begins by *reducing all material moves in the market as a whole, and in individual stocks, to a minimum of simple records, and therefrom, anticipating the future of each and all of them from their own present action.*

It reduces stock market investing and trading *to a business* with a scientific, substantial and definite background, as it should be.

Like any other business, it demands the making and preserving of certain plain records and study of them: coupled with their interpretation. As is well known "Practice makes perfect." This Method actually compels practice in an interesting way which soon becomes a habit, and a fascinating hobby. Devotees of the Method, well able to afford assistants, prefer to record the data personally, because of the mental relaxation and the absorbing occupation it affords.

As the Method dispenses, entirely and completely, with the expense and labor involved in buying, owning or keeping bulky memoranda of statistics, fundamentals, corporation reports, balance sheets, earnings statements and the other expensive, cumbersome and elaborate paraphernalia hitherto associated with trading and investing, the substitution of the time and money-saving simple records this Method requires is a consideration.

The Method takes for granted:

(1) That the price of a stock at any given time is its correct valuation up to the instant of purchase and sale (a) by the consensus of opinion of *all* buyers and sellers in the world (b) by the verdict of *all* the forces governing the laws of supply and demand.

(2) That the last price of a stock reflects or crystallizes *everything* known about or bearing on it from its first sale on the Exchange (or prior), up to that time.

(3) That those who know more about it than the observer *cannot* conceal their future intentions regarding it. Their plans will be revealed in time by the stock's subsequent action.

The Point and Figure Method is not a system for beating the stock market. It is the result of rationalization of other methods long used by important market operators. Assuming that the student keeps the records called for, there remains simply a need of understanding the author's mode of reading and interpreting them. The way to go about it with practical illustrations follows. While the work involved is not laborious, and while proficiency may not come easily at first, it presents no insurmountable difficulties. In little time, through study, practice and observation, the habit of right thinking and sound judgment will replace former conjecture and confusion.

It is confidently expected that as a result of condensation and clarity, the reader will commence to appraise the movements, to analyze their reason or motive, and to deduce plausible conclusions that should soon begin to be *more right than wrong*.

Success in trading and investing does not consist in being perfect. This cannot be achieved. *To be more right than wrong is not only the purpose of this Method, but it is the essence of profitable investing and trading.*

To check possible errors, we always use a simple device, namely, stop orders. It is unnecessary to go into details about them here. Their use and purpose is fully described in many works.*

However, with reference to their use, let me comment briefly. In no other enterprise or business is it possible to protect profits, or check losses, with the same facility as it is in the stock and commodity markets, through the use of stop orders. Their use is suggested, except where a form of "averaging" or "pyramiding" is recommended. The mere mention of averaging and pyramiding may cause a shudder and, perhaps, some sympathy for my naivete in hinting that this Method tolerates the process. It not only tolerates averaging and pyramiding at times *but suggests it.*

WEIGHS FORCES OF BUYING AND SELLING

The Method weighs the forces of buying and selling, records the stresses and resistances at all points, gives a wide range of visualization by graphic, lucid records, permits quick and ready comparison of one stock, one group, or several, and/or others. It compels "hewing close to the line" by watching the trend of the market as a whole, individual stocks, and the major groups. *It indicates the best trading and investing opportunities.*

It commands you when to get in, and cautions you when to get out by (a) clear signals to act, or (b) indications where to place stop orders.

The Method assumes that *fractions mean nothing whatever in the long run.* In this respect it is correct.

Your attention is called to Figure 12, page 62, interpreting the action of the N. Y. Times averages, June to December 1929. Here was a drop from 311 to 165 within three months, clearly indicated by the Method long in advance, without the aid of fractions. Such a decline in these staid averages, the most violent within such a short time in market history, reducing individual stock quotations to modest *percentages* of former prices, obviously did not result from fractional influences, nor from daily trading *regulated by fractions.*

---

*See "Stop Orders. How to use them for Profit" by Owen Taylor (Stock Market Publications)

The Method does not dispense with the value or virtue of tape reading. It aids that science, by insisting that mere fractions do not count in the long run.   It emphasizes the value of the *full figures* that the averages or individual stocks reach up to, or recede from. It relies upon the**professional hypothesis that those who, in the last analysis, ultimately make or break the market - the public - think first, in terms of full figures , not in fractions, and, second, in terms of the *natural* ciphers and round digits like 10, 15, 20, 25, 30 etc.

As to the latter, the Method is logically adjusted.

Average public opinion as to a price objective is always expressed in these most convenient *natural* round figures. It is a human trait so to do. The omission of a couple of cents from a price tag is a well known device. To make an article appear less expensive, the merchant draws attention away from *round figures*. That is why a $1.98 price tag sells more goods than a $2.00 one.

The Author will show how the Method ignores mere salesmanship by insisting upon full figures only, with emphasis upon the crucial milestones - the tens and fives.

II. ADVANTAGES OF THIS METHOD OVER OTHERS

There are certain definite advantages of this Method, measured largely by the elimination of non-essentials, condensation and speed in obtaining results. These are stressed to reassure the student. A great number of parts and ponderous accessories do not improve the perfect machine.   They oftimes interfere with its efficiency.   The Point and Figure Method has minimized these detractions.   Here in summary manner may be mentioned some outstanding advantages, for the more useful purpose of clearly indicating what is *not* necessary.

The Method practically *dispenses* with, (a) statistics, (b) fundamentals, (c) values - real, absent or presumed, (d) news - past, present or future, (e) necessity for impulsive action, (f) decisions based upon conjecture, (g) compulsion to interpret or determine the effect before the cause, (h) confusion of mental processes, in the task of prematurely anticipating or discounting coming events.

The Method *provides*, among other things, these outstanding advantages, (a) clarity in reading its graphic records, (b) simplicity and neatness in keeping them, (c) logical, clean-cut patterns easier to read, interpret and remember, (d) higher speed in adequately recording all data, (e) reduction of data to chronicle material facts only, (f) alternative adaptation of the graphic memoranda in several forms for studying, interpreting and checking, (g) prolific means of checking and testing these vivid facts, their implications, motives and the probable con-

**A better term than "insider" since it includes pools, and major independent operators having no connection with the inside — presumably the corporation itself, or its market sponsors.

clusions resulting therefrom.

WHY VOLUME IS UNNECESSARY

The Method dispenses entirely with the recording of the volume of sales, preferring to leave such details for good reasons to other forms of charting price movements.

The factor of volume, applied to the market as a whole and individual stocks in particular, is an important one. It has its proper place elsewhere. We do not, in this particular Method, rely upon an irregular factor such as this. Volume is susceptible to manipulation and deceit to an unusual degree. Here is the reason.

Volume is not always a true index of supply and demand in the group of common stock equities totaling 1265 stock issues now listed on the New York Stock Exchange. They have different characteristics, varying price planes, utterly different capital structures and wide disparity in the number of shares outstanding. Changing tastes in speculation effect activity in individual groups of stocks. Oftimes, despite activity, lack of balance may swerve judgment through artificial price washing in stocks in the following category: (a) too low priced to serve as barometers (b) too heavily capitalized to assist in judging the trend (c) too popular to indicate true professional or public participation (d) too volatile, closely held, sensitive, or too easily influenced independently.

For these and other good tested reasons the advocates of this Method and adherents to these records avoid volume *altogether*.

FACILITY OF THIS METHOD

However, having regard to the time element, and the desirability of recording, judging and anticipating the possible duration of the immediate, intermediate, and main moves, we are able by this Method to record, read and interpret the *monthly* and *seasonal* movements in groups and individual stocks with great facility.

We can visualize the broad moves in various forms at a glance. Our surveys are rapid and precise, the ground is covered with a minimum of effort. We concern ourselves with nothing but the *facts*, using a minimum of data which in the making has really covered a good deal of ground. We know, for example, that a move within range of 50 to 55 in a day with a close at 54, may have traveled a laborious or an easy path, depending whether its ingredients were 50, 51, 50, 51, 52, 51, 52, 53, 52, 53, 52, 51, 52, 53, 54, 55, 54, 53, 52, 53, 54 or whether it came 50, 51, 52, 53, 52, 53, 54, 55, 54, 53, 54, 55, 54, 55, 54, 53, 54, 55, 54. The latter is, to the experienced analyst, the more bullish formation than the former. In the previous case, even without information as the volume of transactions at the lower or higher prices, a glance tells us that the stock was in supply up to 53, with ample offerings below 55. In the latter case, the factor of scarcity is evident by the ease with which the stock quickly reached 55, and its ability to rebound to within a point of the apex of the move, and to hold its gain to the close.

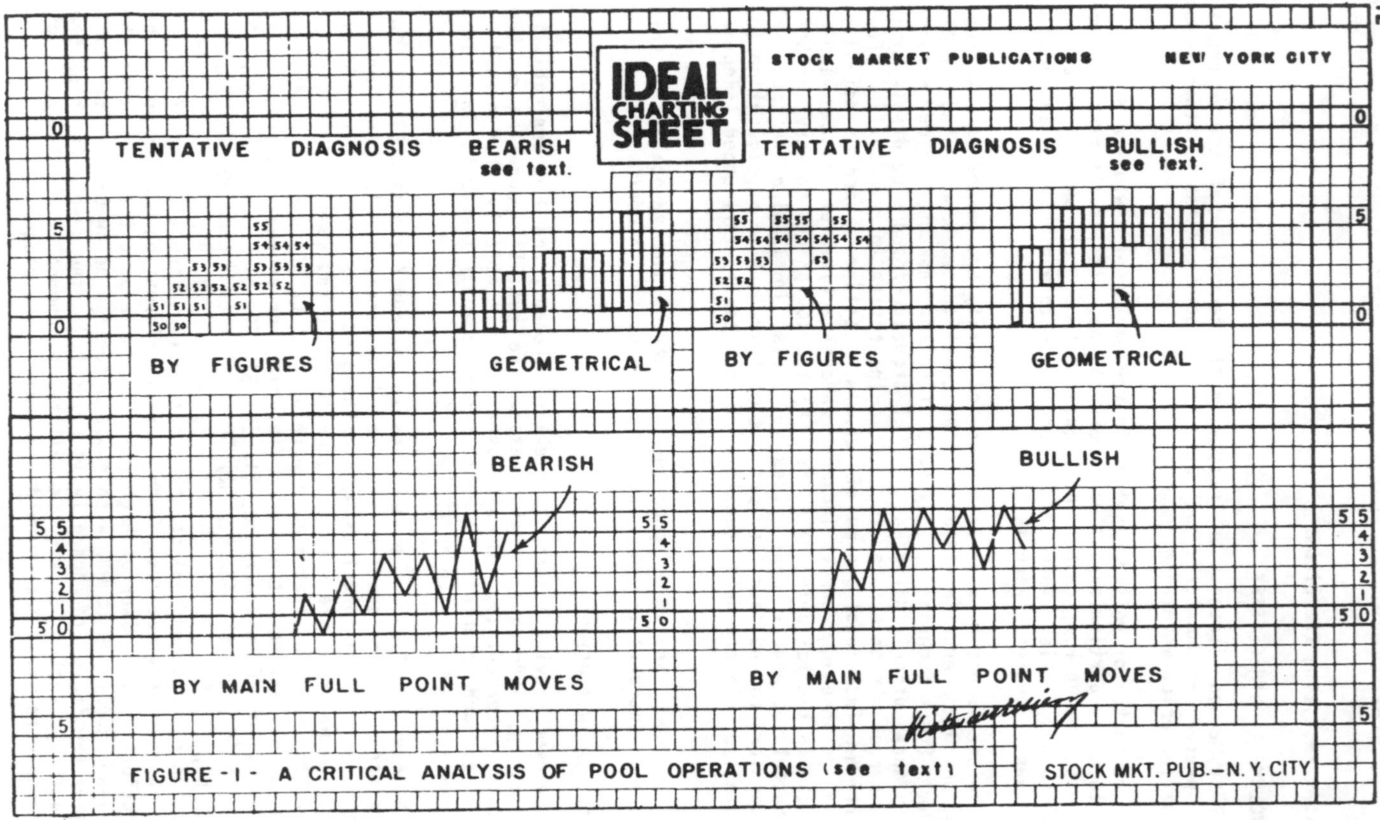

STOCK MARKET PUBLICATIONS   NEW YORK CITY

IDEAL CHARTING SHEET

TENTATIVE DIAGNOSIS   BULLISH
see text.

TENTATIVE DIAGNOSIS   BEARISH
see text.

GEOMETRICAL

BY FIGURES

GEOMETRICAL

BY FIGURES

BULLISH

BEARISH

BY MAIN FULL POINT MOVES

BY MAIN FULL POINT MOVES

FIGURE - I - A CRITICAL ANALYSIS OF POOL OPERATIONS (see text)   STOCK MKT. PUB.—N. Y. CITY

This demonstration is subject to qualifications, depending on the methods of the pool operating in this particular stock.

OPERATORS VARY THEIR PLANS

Certain operators prefer to depress a stock and to make it look weak when its objective is higher prices. Other operators, whose tactics are bolder and more open, do not hesitate to bid up, take stock, and continue a more spectacular course. The former may be considered more conservative, clever or cunning. The latter accomplish their purpose by daring methods that also have a wide public appeal, through the public, board room traders, brokerage house partners, customers' men etc.

Nothing succeeds like success. The spectacular operators believe in advertising their success. Fireworks in a stock, with consequent lively tape action in hundreds of board rooms, the excited gossip, free advertising in dozens of leading newspapers and substantial plus signs, not only appeal to the courageous operators, but really attract a great following. It is a matter of *test* and *taste* as to which works best.

However, the building up of subsequent point and figure work, following an unusual move like the one illustrated, *will really tell the story.* This type of move is a signal to get ready to act - for profit, either on the upside or on the downside. The alert student waits for these unusual demonstrations because they afford opportunities to be prepared to take a position in the market, one way or other - long or short. Important action usually seems bound to follow.

This charted movement, here illustrated, refers to no particular stock, but furnishes a rather extreme example of what has happened in a single day, in a single stock, and, what is likely to occur again.

By first recording and, then, studying such a real analysis of a movement when it occurs, with well-founded belief that it is almost *bound to be repeated* in exaggerated or modified form the next day, the day after, and probably for days or weeks later, even though a period of calm or consolidation may intervene, we begin to realize the significance of the homely old phrase "figures do not lie."

III.   WHY THIS METHOD IS SUPERIOR TO INSIDE INFORMATION

By this Method the so-called insider has no better advantage than the outsider - the public.

The market is made or unmade by demand and supply. True, major interests pools and large operators can accelerate or retard a movement, temporarily. They can start something by large scale buying or selling, particularly in inactive, closely held issues. But, they can no more buck the trend in the last analysis than we can. *They* must also yield to pressure and resistance. *They* often make mistakes. *They* take large losses at times. *They* cannot quickly reverse their positions

with the same facility as can the average person. *They* are by no means
infallible.

This Method records the consolidation of actual facts, *the price.*

This *price* compresses into a single digit or cipher every known or
unknown fact or factor *to date.* What more can anybody wish to know?

Authentic inside information must not and cannot be disclosed.
It would wreck costly plans.   If it *is* disclosed, it is no longer inside.   It is then not worth knowing, obviously, for it immediately becomes common property, in the class of a peddled tip - *the most expensive mis*-information in Wall Street.

The force of combined public sentiment is back of each and every
transaction.   Millions of people comprise the public. Their inaction
may calm the tides of speculation, and cause a normally turbulent sea
look like a millpond for awhile. *That* would be no excuse for navigating
around Cape Hatteras in a canoe! When these millions decide to act, or
rather, show tentative signs of activity, the alert major interests,
pools, bankers or substantial operators may endeavor to *anticipate* broader, more universal action, by initial buying or selling that may or may
not act as a self-starter, and encourage a following - in the same
direction.   Whatever the insiders do cannot be accomplished in secret;
their *transactions must appear* on the tape.   The tape and newspaper
publicizes all! The nature of the latter makes it everybody's property.

This Method calmly records the meat of such transactions, the full
figures, just as the insider does - whether it goes on his books,
through his bank, or on his charts. The student of this Method doing the
same thing is *also* an insider.   The hard-working student is a *better*
insider, has a better opportunity, and is better able through smaller,
more compact commitments to reverse or close trades, than the heavy cal-
iber professional pool operator, banker or any other popular conception
of insider who has gone ahead confidently, and has embarked upon large -
scale commitments on opinions, information and belief, plus hope.

Again we emphasize, *the stock market is a business.*   It is potentially and naturally a more profitable business for interests with large
capital, operating *intelligently,* than for the small investor or trader
with a few hundred, or few thousand dollars in securities. Conversely, it is far more dangerous and unprofitable, if not potentially quite
disastrous, for major interests to be caught pursuing a course dia-
metrically opposed to, ultimate public sentiment, or probable action.
Yet, dollar for dollar of investment considered, the outsider can show
a better proportion of profits on limited capital than the capitalist, -
through greater freedom of action and less need for cautious movement.
This Method warns long in advance of a probable change in such sentiment,
and the average investor or trader can act appropriately - by taking a
neutral position, a reversed position, or, by placing strategic stop
orders.

The major interests cannot do this if they have miscalculated their
fundamentals, or have disregarded them, or have overstayed the limits
of prudence, or, as can happen unexpectedly, if the great tides of specu-

lation change from millpond calm, or a clear ebbtide course, into an overwhelming hurricane overnight.

Do they not understand the basic principles of investing, trading and speculating as well as this author, and as well as indicated by this Method? Some probably do, and others do not. Those immense major interests who do understand, cannot always take advantage of their knowledge, nor can they always do, nor care to do as they would like to do, at the psychological time.

In this connection, it is worthy to note this comment from "The Financial World," June 14, 1933 (L.G.'s column, page 573): "With all the power Morgan supposedly possessed, and with all the information available, the house lost tremendously during the depression, indicating that it was composed simply of human beings and not the supermen the newspapers try to picture. When asked for an explanation for this loss, Morgan answered 'Who has not made mistakes in the last five years?'....This confession should make others realize that if judgment in high places can err, the individual can scarcely avoid mistakes." (Italics are mine - Author)

The House of Morgan took a depreciation of around a quarter billion dollars in the depression panic, as revealed before the June 1933 Senate Investigation. It was neither a mistake nor an error, with due respect to America's foremost banker, and with real appreciation of the kindly tolerance of* Mr. Louis Guenther. The naive explanation of Mr. Morgan is whimsical but oracular. It is couched in sincere, modest language worthy of a gentlemanly tradition noblesse oblige.

THE REAL TRUTH

The truth is, as the Method insists, there came a time in 1929 after Labor Day, when it was prudent because of dangerous technical market conditions to get out and stay out. The five point chart of the Times Averages, Figure 12, indicated it. Fundamentals dictated it. It is also a basic rule that when the entire world is long of stocks, and when the public is in - hook, line and sinker - it is time for the prudent to get out.

Did not all the major well-informed interests, as well as the Morgans well know this? They probably did, but they could not act physically, justly, or fairly. Other major insiders were inside, and could not and, dared not get outside. When a mere percentage of belated forced liquidation was begun from 305-300 Times Averages , the drop of 140 points in averages attested the fact that, the prior unbridled general speculation had created a super-Frankenstein, perilous to turn loose, indiscreet to unchain, and ultimately impossible to hold in leash anyhow.

Suppose the reader was an insider or had inside information available in early Fall 1929. What would have been the advantage? The

*Publisher and Editor-in-Chief "The Financial World"

foremost financial interests admitted mistakes.   A well-informed authority believes they   erred.   Is there any certainty of or assurance
against the reliability, or otherwise   of inside opinions, judgment, or
information in the future?

There is no such assurance and there never will be.

Therefore, it is best to rely upon logical judgment, proceeding
from analytical conclusions, based upon the *facts* the figures and pro-
babilities, direction of trend , all of which are summarized for you by
this Method.

Inasmuch as market knowledge, by and large, is *not* an exact science,
errors of judgment, interpretation and, hence, conclusions may occur infrequently. The most positive indications may be reversed almost momen-
tarily by unforeseen, *momentous* influences, favorable or adverse. Usually,
months ahead events are anticipated, discounted by major interests, by
buying or selling. Each point up or down reflects these conditions.
Each move is inside information. A 3 point move talks louder. A 5
point move shouts.

But, they are the moves of human beings not of   supermen,
who *hope* to be right. Your own composite picture should disclose best
the way they are moving, and *when*, and *how*. It does not give reasons.
It has no occasion to excuse or explain itself.   The Method advises
you to read, mark, learn and inwardly digest. Elsewhere, Figure 9,
page 54, we show why you can now and for evermore, dispense with inside information.

This Method and yourself, duly fortified with the figures, can
be and should be the best informed insider.

IV. DATA REQUIRED FOR PROPER APPLICATION OF THIS METHOD

All the data needed can and should be reduced to graphic charts,
simple to compile, record, handle, and preserve.

This does not mean that the Method is a *system* of playing by
charts.   It has no such basis in fact.   I should say that if anybody
has a good enough memory to recall thousands of changing figures, in
hundreds of stocks, in a dozen averages, over a period of several years,
he can absolve himself from the labor of keeping charts.

Much uniformed and ignorant derision has been leveled at serious
market students who keep charts.   The Method calls for their careful
compilation and preservation. Who is right?

A meaningless prejudice has been built up against *market* charts by
other than market experts, who know nothing whatever about such charts,
who have failed to understand them, and who upon inquiry have usually lost
money in the stock market. It is our firm conviction also, that certain
operators with possible ulterior motives, have fostered prejudicial pro-

paganda, and encouraged ridicule, by such catchwords as chart fiends, to *discourage* the use of charts, and *encourage* blind speculation by dead reckoning, or guesswork.

Certain successful tape readers, with extraordinary memories, rely solely upon experience and an uncanny judgment that amounts to a sixth sense. However, the majority lost thousands before they made hundreds. Certain investors and traders achieve a measure of success through a modicum of data, some judgment, and a favorable ebb tide that they have wisely, or through fortunate choice, elected to go along with.

It has been said, without authority, carelessly, and through unconscious mimicry, "The market is an unbeatable game." As the entire statement rests on a false premise, those who know their logic, law, or geometry will instantly rule that dogma out of court.

The market is not a game. It is a mart for evaluating, bartering, buying, and selling commodities, stocks, bonds, grain, hides, silver, oil, tin and/or equities, and goods of all kinds. In emphasizing the importance of compiling data and keeping charts, the value of such records should be as obvious as the merchant's books, or the captain's log. To ridicule their value, to discourage their use, and to regard the meeting place, where the opinions of tens of millions is finally focused into *a single figure*, the price, as a *game*, is crude impertinence.

Our defence of recorded data by means of graphic charts however compels assent to the viewpoint that the average, *uniformed* participant, call him trader, speculator, or market player has a slender chance of holding his own for any great length of time. Even the *investor* long or short pull, conservative or daring, takes grave risks without the material assistance of a good method. That good investments can shrink to ten per cent of former, known, or book values is generally realized by now. Can apparently sound investments be safeguarded against a 75 to 90 per cent depreciation in the future? The answer is, yes.

The Point and Figure Method through its recording data, once thoroughly understood, should prevent depreciation of such cyclonic force in the future. Records are essential: charts, graphic records if you please! Leading financial and business journals publish and esteem them. You can do no less.

ESSENTIAL DATA

We compile:

(1) *One point charts* of selected stocks and of the more important representative market averages. The more stocks plotted, the better will be the student's conception of the market action.

(2) *Three point charts.* These are a resume of the action as represented by the one points.

(3) *Five point charts.* A further condensation based upon the one points.

The three sets of charts indicated herein may be considered the foundation and background of this Method. However, when no others can be compiled and kept through lack of time or disinclination, these at least must be considered essential. Very good work may be accomplished and valuable deductions continually drawn from the logical interpretations you will make, based upon this data alone.

The foregoing may be deemed sufficient particularly for beginners. However, for the more technically minded specialist who desires to more closely study, analyze and observe the action of this Method, the following additional data kept by us, is highly recommended.

SUPPLEMENTAL DATA

For the average student, investor or trader the foregoing three types of charts are sufficient in themselves for the purpose of judging the technical condition of the market and in analyzing its probable future trend.

As an aid to closer analysis, there is the new half point chart and the hourly and half hourly fluctuations of the Dow-Jones Industrial Index. This is more clearly explained in full detail elsewhere in the book. When you have thoroughly mastered these primary principles, you will then be in a position to advance further in the study of more technical applications of this Method. In another volume to be published later, we will go into greater detail and show how the principles herein outlined can be elaborated upon and used for the purpose of building other important and highly technical charts which will materially aid you in a clearer and more comprehensive analysis of price movements.

APPLICATION OF THIS METHOD TO COMMODITIES

In a subsequent volume the author will show in full detail the application of this Method to the analysis of price movement in commodities, such as wheat, cotton, corn, grain, silver and any other basic commodities dealt in, whose price change fluctuations are recorded on any exchange.

USE AND PURPOSE OF THE RECOMMENDED DATA

(a)   The one point charts provide a relevant picture and, more important, the basic pattern of the actual moves, with fractions omitted. They form the starting point of the Method. They depict the real moves, the action of the tape, not only analytically, but comprehensively, at all times daily, hourly, weekly, monthly, in all plotted stocks and averages. By omitting fractional changes, hundreds of unimportant transactions involved in arriving at actual results may be disregarded. They point the way, without detours.

Whereas there may be hundreds of transactions in a single stock in a single day, the Method only notes full figure relevant and material changes. In the most active stocks, during even 5,000,000 share days or upward, under the greatest stress of manipulation, involving spectacular volumes of sales, the Method only takes cognizance of a mere handful of these full figure material changes.

In a recent climatic session, with volume of sales 6,300,000 shares (June 14, 1933), average material changes in the most active issues were: in the leaders about 5 changes; in the secondary issues about 3 changes. J. I. Case with transactions totalling 290,000 shares recorded 5 changes. However, Allied Chemical with transactions totalling 32,000 shares recorded 8 changes, a most unusual situation which indicates abnormal susceptibility, a delicate position. Contrast this with United Aircraft whose volume exceeded 102,000 with only 2 changes. Montgomery-Ward on transactions totalling above 45,000 shares recorded but one change. General Motors with 127,000 shares transacted also recorded but one change.

(b) *The three point charts* make tentative synopses of the *intermediate trend*. Compiled from one points they give a condensed picture of a mass of detail, over an extended period of time, and record the true measure of the technical advances and declines. They give a broader picture that withdraws the student from too much contemplation of the *daily trading*. The latter is, very often, most deceptive. It furnishes a trial balance as it were. A more truthful picture as to how the market stands at any given time is furnished from the three points. It is an invaluable *intermediate trend* indicator, once facility is acquired in reading and interpreting its implications.

(c) *The five point charts*, also compiled from the one points guide us in our observation of the broad *main trend*. Because these only take note of the expansive moves, they furnish a more reliable index of the true position, and manipulation of higher priced, closely held, more volatile, wider moving issues. It is most difficult, if not impossible, to judge the objectives of certain stocks in this category, from day to day, or to detect accumulation, marking up, pauses, congestion points, distribution or culmination, without them. The precision and value of such a compilation may be judged from Figure 12, page 62, showing the action of the N.Y. Times Averages, June-December 1929, and the accompanying explanation. For the investor and long range semi-investor the five point compilation is recommended, not only in the special issues referred to, but also for detecting the direction and moves of the averages and/or individual stocks that are of interest to the student.

THE METHOD SUBSTITUTES FOR TAPE READING

(d) *The half-point charts* are suitable for many purposes, and are particularly adapted for recording hourly and half-hourly changes of the market as a whole. A more reliable and closer analysis of averages than by means of one points is made available by plotting market fluctuations from *hour to hour*. This, fortunately, does not involve sitting in a broker's office, nor watching the tape. The Dow-Jones Averages are printed hourly over the news ticker, published in the "Wall Street Journal" daily, and furnished in log form by reputable advisory services. Those who need the figures during the day may obtain them by telephone from any brokers' office about fifteen minutes after the opening, each hour, and after the close. However, this Method *does not recognize the absolute need* for such prompt, close action. Records made a day later will be sufficient in the long run. Pending the compilation of data, stop orders should take care of unexpected reversals, contrary to trend indications, which may occur during the day.

(e) One point charts of full figure fluctuations of an index compiled from five active leaders are recommended as a better, and more prompt indicator than the averages published hourly. The one point of five actives is useful to the trader, the tape reader, and those who have trading or ticker facilities. whether in brokerage headquarters, in the office, or home. Recording important tape action as affecting five leaders in as many groups, an unusual check-up is afforded, giving clues to the probable direction of many immediate moves. "As Steel goes, so goes the market" has been an old trading rule. The author is not commited to this axiom. We prefer to be guided by the action of five leaders - not by a single stock.

Conscientiously kept, this picture, built up, day by day, will eventually provide an invaluable piece of data which the author has found clear and free of the confusion often surrounding the obscure contradictory, and mixed movements of hundreds of stocks, comprising the market as a whole.

(f) The immediate trend outline charts of ten selected leaders are entirely optional, and suggested merely for the purpose of comparison and study, until proficiency is gained in reading the regular one point charts at a glance. Any ten active leaders may be selected, but they should be real leaders, preferably those that move widely, with many changes, having an influence on the market, such as, for example, American Telephone, Allied Chemical, Case, Auburn, Union Pacific, U. S. Steel, Consolidated Gas, etc.   Temperamental stocks like Case and Auburn are included because they furnish important guides to the speculative aspect of the market as a whole, irrespective whether the student cares to trade or invest in them or not.

(g) The intermediate trend outline charts of ten leaders and averages, by three point moves, is also to be used for the purpose of giving another viewpoint, a new picture somewhat detached from the details of their origin - the one points. They give a broad picture and provide a more familiar pattern chart of stocks and averages. Recording merely technical advances or declines at a glance, a ready method of building up intermediate and main trend lines is thus afforded from such graphic, visualization in simple, easy form. The simplicity and possible value to the student of such a chart is evident from Figure 4, page 37.   Ten leaders and selected averages should be kept in this form for ready reference.

(h) The main trend outline charts of ten leaders and selected averages, are compiled from the five point moves only. The N. Y. Times Averages June-December 1929 page 62, shows such a compilation, in proper form. In our experience, it has proven extremely difficult, if not impossible, to judge the main trend, with any degree of even approximate accuracy, without such a compilation.

This group of charts, together with (c) should be regarded as the real compass, pointing true North, and a reliable guide for longer range commitments of all kinds. Naturally, the trend lines which can be compiled from the data of this group of charts, will be a truer and more reliable picture of the broader, and longer outlook. Charts (c) and (d) are moreover, reliable guides throughout a complete market from bear to bull market, and reverse allowing the market ample leeway to advance and decline in the ordinary course of its ultimate price path, *without causing the student to lose his main bearings.*

V. HOW TO PREPARE AND COLLATE THE NEEDED DATA

It is a great help to keep all the data neatly, uniformly, clearly and compactly. The author has devoted thought to this aspect because to do otherwise, as we know from past experience, is a handicap on time, energy and nerves. We wish to concentrate on study of the *problems* presented, at convenient ease, with a minimum of manual effort.

For this purpose specially devised charting sheets are available , which we now recommend and use exclusively. These are of medium weight, good quality, opaque 8½" x 11", loose-leaf sheets for conventional 12" x 10" 3-ring binders. They are convenient to insert, change around, or remove. We use different colored stock for I, 3, and 5 points. The special ruling, novel arrangements for digits and ciphers for reading at a glance, negligible possibility of error, and instant indication of exact price, make these unusually valuable accessories of the Method. All of the charts reproduced herein were drafted on these special sheets. It is sufficient to make the records with a good quality, hard pencil. An assistant, with more time, and taking pride in the work, would prefer to use india ink and a steel drafting pen.

From thirty minutes to one hour daily will be found sufficient for recording all *essential* data. The supplementary material takes a little longer at first, and may be done any time during the day or evening after the essential ground work has been completed. It is important, if market commitments are to be made same day, to complete the one points first. In your loose-leaf binders these white sheets are kept on the top, below are the threes and fives, different colors ; or, they may be kept in a different book. The same applies to supplementary data. The arrangement must depend upon personal preference, convenience, amount of data the student can keep, and his objective. We impose no arbitrary arrangement on you.

Business men, capitalists, institutions, major operators, or larger traders will find it a paying investment to let an assistant study the manner of charting and keeping the records, passing on the finished work for study and analysis. Any intelligent assistant, young man or woman, after a little preliminary study of what is required, can keep all the memoranda adequately.

We recommend compiling a minimum of 50 active and leading stocks.

They should include the most prominent, and this number is advisable, whether or not the student is interested in any or all of them. Personal selections, additions, or substitutions will normally follow the trend of such a cross-section of the market.   In addition, the three main group averages like the Dow-Jones 30 Industrials, 20 Rails and 20 Utilities should be kept. They are widely known and quoted.

A greater number of individual stocks could be kept to still greater advantage, say up to 100 issues. The N. Y. Times 50 stocks and Herald-Tribune 100 stocks are additional barometric averages, widely quoted and relied upon. If at all possible, time permitting, it will be found worth while to compile and own the entire set of 100 individual stocks and five charts of averages in one-point form. This furnishes a valuable guide to a substantial cross-section, about 10 per cent, of the whole market. As five-point changes occur infrequently, no great additional effort is attached to that work.

While at first glance this may look like *work*, however, let us call attention to the fact that the public's great losses in *every* major cycle change has usually been occasioned by *lack of work* marketwise.   "The drones must die!"   Investment and trading is a business proposition, first, last and always. It should be conducted along those lines, if ultimate success be desired. The work is interesting and the needed materials are inexpensive. The compensation for conscientious effort is far out of proportion to the labor involved.

CLARIFYING THE PRINCIPLES INVOLVED

In any given stock call it XYZ*, we begin at the last full flat figure. For example, between 34 1/8 to 35 7/8, neither 34 flat nor 36 flat has been made. Therefore, our starting point is 35, and we make a cross at that figure. If the stock has already advanced from 33 *plus,* *83 1/8 or better and up through 34 and 35 plus, the figure 34 would precede 35. When the stock reaches 36 flat or better, we *record the 36 and then we make no changes until - the stock declines to 35 flat or below , or advances to 37 flat or above. It is clear there would be no change at 35 1/8, or at 35 7/8. No matter how often a new full figure change occurs daily, it is recorded. The Method records all fluctations occuring in *full figure changes,* and *not in time.*

Assume that the stock now declines to 34 7/8, it has *passed down and through* 35, which latter figure we record. It makes a low of 34 1/8, no change, and closes 36 1/8. Our new addition would be 36 since it made the latter full figure, or better. Let us presume it opens next day at 37 7/8, goes to 38, declines to 36 7/8, and advances to 39¼. Our new figures are 37, 38, 37, 38, 39. Thereafter, it hovers between 38 3/8 to 39 7/8, no full figure changes, rallies to 40, we record 40, dips to 38 7/8, we record 39, rises to 40 7/8, we record 40, and closes 37½ on a straight sell off.   Having thus *passed down through* 39 and 38 we record these figures. Next day, opening is 37 flat, we record 37, it then declines to 34½, we record 36, 35, and the rally is to 39¼. We record 36, 37, 38, 39 because the price path has reached, passed through and made, all these full figures.

---

*See Figure 2, page 23.

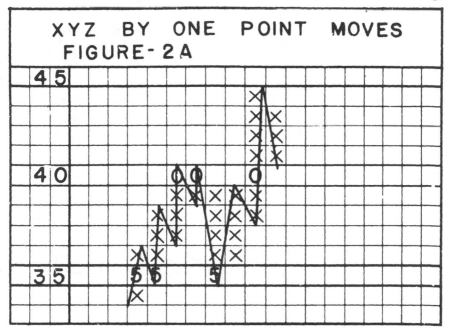

XYZ BY ONE POINT MOVES
FIGURE-2A

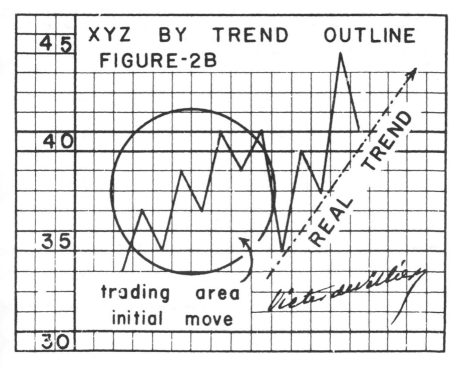

XYZ BY TREND OUTLINE
FIGURE-2B

REAL TREND

trading area
initial move

Thus, it is clear, than an extreme fluctuation from any full figure plus 1/8 to 7/8 is no change, and that, from full figure plus 1/8, to next full figure plus 7/8, is simply a *one point change* so far as this Method is concerned.

To illustrate by progression of preceding figures, last full recorded figure was 39. It next rallies to 39 7/8 no change declines to 39 no change; we have that figure already , and drops to 38½. We *cannot* record a change here until 38 flat or less is made. It will be noted that we have disregarded a movement of 1⅜ points, and will continue doing so because to this Method such a move is not significant. It is merely a minor fluctuation. However, in this case, another eighth down to 38 flat alters the picture, and we record 38.

Therefore, hundreds of points in total fractional variations may be disregarded and thrown into the discard by this Method, because it says:- *Fractional fluctuations do not count unless they complete full figure variations.*

By this means, days of apparent activity, large volume, violent fractional changes within 1⅜ points range, general trading excitement in a stock may mean little, or nothing whatever, to those who adhere to the Point and Figure Method. Unless *a new full flat figure* is reached, it is never recorded and is disregarded by the Method.

GAPS NOT RECORDED

An important feature of this Method is the fact that it does not recognize gaps. Whether the gap is created through the stock failing to travel regularly by fractions, whether it pursues the erratic course of skipping points between sales as many volatile stocks will do , or whether it opens up or down, no matter how radically or violently , this Method presumes for all practical purposes that *the transgression or irregularity will be corrected in time.* The Method also aims to ignore temporary irregularities of this calibre, which do not materially affect eventual results, or the real price path, over a given period of time.

Let us see, then, how such gaps are handled by the Method, and the compilation of its data.

We continue with XYZ, whose last price is 38 and is so recorded. It becomes inactive. Some bullish news is printed unexpectedly on the news ticker. "XYZ dividend raised from $2 to $4." Somebody wishes to buy 1,000 shares quickly. Market is 38½ - 40. The buyer takes it at the market. It comes 40 over the tape, skipping 39. It *passed up through 39* according to the Method. We, therefore, record 39, 40. It closes 41½, we record 41. Bid and asked price at close is 41½ - 41¾.

XYZ opens next day 43½. Lower offerings disappeared before the opening, evidently. Therefore, it *passed up through 42*, made 43, we record both , reached 44 flat we record this , and closes 42¼ regularly, *passing both* by fractions *through 43* we record this . Next day opening transaction is 40 7/8 on early news that higher dividend rate $4 is not to be taken as a permanent policy. The Method ignores the gap as well as the news, presumes the stock *passed down through 42* and 41, which figures we also record impartially.

The detached, cool manner in which the Method and the records ignore gaps are justified, by the work ultimately built up on the three and five point charts. The Method is indeed broad and tolerant.

At this stage, our one point chart will appear as is shown, with graphic chart on right showing direction of the fluctuations.

EXPLANATION AND INTERPRETATION OF GRAPH - Figure 2 - Page 23

From inception of the move, 34 to first mark up at 40 shorts run in, and too much company attracted. Five point drop to 35 deters a following and attracts new short interest. Sharp 4 point rally to 39, I point decline, bullish, and a 6 point rise to 44 does not by a 3 point decline to 41 - half way, - cancel bullish implication.

VI. APPROVED METHOD OF PREPARING POINT AND FIGURE CHARTS

Attention is again called to Figure 2, Page 23, depicting the one point action of XYZ. The one point is the starting base of this Method. It will pay to follow the moves, point by point.

Beginning at 34 an x is placed there for a start, immediately below the digit 5, horizontal line. We use x's because of known convenience, rapidity and clarity. On rise to 35 place a 5 above our 34x. It is advisable to use the figure 5 and 0 where these digits and ciphers occur. We figure moves in short cycles of fives and tens, each cipher being another important milestone as it were.

On rise to 36, we continue vertically by placing an x above 35. Decline to 35 calls for another digit, 5 to the right of and below 36. Rise to 36, 37, 38 calls for continuation of vertical formation by x's as indicated. Decline to 37 calls for an x in square to right immediately below 38, nearest space.   Recovery to 38 is indicated by an x above 37 continuing vertical formation, and further rise to 39 and 40 is indicated by x for 39 and cipher 0 for 40 directly vertical and above 38.

It will be noted, thus far, that the Method condenses and follows a logical course.   Next dip to 39 calls for an x immediately to right of and below 40, nearest square, and advance to 40 is indicated by another cipher 0 above 39. Straight decline from 39 to 35 is charted by x in the 9 square immediately to right under 40.   No mistake is possible because it is the nearest space not used, x's for 8, 7 and 6 follow, with a 5 in the digit space.   The straight advance to 36, 37, 38, 39 calls for continuation of the vertical formation to the right, as always, beginning from nearest 6 square to completion of rally to the 9 square --all indicated by x's.   Decline to 38 following is recorded by an x immediately to the right, while ensuing rise to 44 is simply recorded by continuing vertical direction of movement immediately above 39, by the usual 0, at 40 and x's at 41, 42, 43, 44. Decline, straight to 41 calls for x's immediately to right.

PRICE PATH AND TREND OUTLINE

The thin line superimposed upon the x's, digits and ciphers in the illustration shows clearly the way the symbols are recorded:- *the price path*. The immediate trend outline in same illustration is merely an outline without symbols, giving a more understandable picture of *the same move*.

Attention is called to the semi-catapult position of the stock at 41. Here, after considerable manipulation, and confusing moves all resistance is overcome, at a new high point, compelling a tentative diagnosis--trend is now up. Higher support after double bottom at 35 also confirms this indication. The real move has begun at an average of 38. . Obviously, the place to stop the stock is 37 flat remembering the theory of the Method - *to disregard fractions*.

The foregoing explains the proper way to record one point moves by important intermediate swings that are peculiarly related to inside manipulation, and public psychology. To summarize, we use x's for facility, and the 5s and Os to designate real stages of the movement.

PURPOSE OF FIGURE CHARTS

Figure charts are made in exactly the same manner, by using the full single figure in place of an x, in the proper square. The author, by long use, has become accustomed to the point Method, rather than the figure Method. Both are good. Many students react more promptly to the picture of the figures, with constant repetition of certain figures or groups of them, furnishing a rapid summary of probable direction and motives. Reproducing the same graph in figure form, appearance would be as follows:

```
        45                            45
                      4                               x
                      3 3                             x x
ONE                   2 2                             x x       ONE
POINT                 1 1                             x x       POINT
CHART   40        0 0       0         40        0 0       0     CHART
BY                9 9 9 9 9                  x x x x x           CONVEN-
FIGU.ES           8 8   8 8 8               x x   x x x         TIONAL
                  7 7   7 7                 x x   x x
                6 6     6 6               x x     x x
        35      5 5     5             35  5 5     5
                4                         x
```

Over a rather long period of time, the repetition of clear figures, their vivid impression on the mind and aid to memory, is counted an advantage by those who prefer them.   The figure type of chart is older than the point type, the former being considered old-fashioned and the latter modern. Experimentation alone will tell you which type will suit your purpose best.   Asked to give a decision, the author would favor the charts he uses most - the modern point charts.

COMPILING THREE POINT CHARTS

Having learned how to handle the one point moves, and make the required charts as indicated, it is a simple matter to compile three point charts.   These must be compiled from the one point data already plotted, and in no other manner.

Three point charts ignore every fluctuation excepting *three full* point moves in either direction.   A 1 or 2 point rise or decline is ignored.   Anything below 2 7/8 points or above 2 7/8 points is noticed and charted - obviously. For 3 point charts a move must be 3 full points, and no less.

Using the above movement, a range of 34 to 44 for illustration , the move from 34 to 36 calls for no entry.   Decline to 35 not recorded. But the rise to 37 is 3 full points from the low 34 hence our first formation, record 34 straight up to 37. As the move continues to 38, we also record an 8.   Decline to 37 is ignored, only 1 point, but rise to 40 calls for completion of the intermediate move, so we insert a 9 and 0.   We ignore decline to 39 and rise to 40, 1 point each, but must record decline from 40 to 35, a 5 point move because it is 3 points or more.   We, therefore, record 9, 8, 7, 6 and 5, following our rule to record the full swing in same direction.   Next follows a 4 point move - 36, 7, 8, 9, record this.   A, 1 point decline, 38 and 1 point rise, 39 follows - - ignore it.   Then comes a 5 point rise to 44 which we must record, 3 points or over as shown, followed by a final 3 point decline, also shown.   The picture appears thus:

	45		4					45		x			
			3	3						x	x		
THREE			2	2						x	x		THREE
POINT			1	1						x	x		POINT
CHART	40		0	0			40		0	0		CHART
BY		9	9	9				x	x	x		CONVEN-
FIGURES		8	8	8				x	x	x		TIONAL
		7	7	7				x	x	x		
		6	6	6				x	x	x		
	35		5	5			35		5	5		
			4							x		

Elsewhere we have analyzed the movements of Western Union by one and three point moves. By comparing the two graphic charts, and the entries recorded, it will be a simple matter to check whether the reader has fully grasped the principles involved as illustrated by the text and figures.

COMPILING FIVE POINT CHARTS

Five point charts are *also* compiled from the one point moves. They ignore everything except fluctuations of five full points or more, but not less. As such broader moves are less frequent, the labor is simplified proportionately. However, wide, fast moving issues, of which Allied Chemical, Union Pacific, American Telephone, Case Threshing, American Can, U. S. Steel preferred, and similar descriptions are good examples in the recently bullish March-June 1933 upswing, furnish more information by five point charts. It is our opinion that it would be more difficult to appraise their intermediate or main direction moves without the use of five point charts.

The principles involved in plotting three point moves are identical for five point variations. Again using the graphs for illustration and demonstration of the Method, the following is our procedure:

XYZ moved from 34 to 36, then a 1 point decline, no record. A 3 point advance, no action, a 1 point decline, no action, and a further 3 point rise to 40. Our first full 5 point move is at 39, which we record as also the next figure - 40. We ignore the fluctuations 39 and 40 following and simply note the first 5 point decline from high of 40. It comes down to 35, that we record. Thence follows a 4 point rise, ignored, a 1 point decline, no record, thence a sheer advance to 44. As our last complete record stood at 35, we have waited for a full 5 point figure change which comes at 40, we record this. The rise continues to 44, so we add 41, 42, 43, 44 by progressing the move in straight up vertical direction, as explained for 1 and 3 points . The subsequent decline of 3 points - 43, 42, 41, - calls for no further action. The picture then appears thus:

```
        45                                 45
                          4                              x
                          3                              x
FIVE                      2                              x          FIVE
POINT                     1                              x          POINT
CHART         40        0   0            40        0   0            CHART
BY                      9 9 9                      x x x            CONVEN-
FIGURES                 8 8 8                      x x x            TIONAL
                        7 7 7                      x x x
                        6 6 6                      x x x
              35        5 5              35        5 5
                        4                                x
```

WHERE THE DATA IS AVAILABLE

The tape reader can get the full figure changes directly from the tape. That is where they are recorded in the first instance, and they are authentic, unless corrected immediately, as is usually the case when error occurs.

However, few people have the opportunity to watch the tape so closely. It is almost a professional and trained job to follow the fluctuations and record even the full figure changes in 50 to 100 stocks during an active market. Fortunately, this is entirely unnecessary for the purpose of this Method, and rather a hindrance to the acquisition of calm judgment on the part of the student.

All metropolitan daily papers give the material price changes. In the case of a great number of stocks that are not particularly active, nor too wide-moving, a fairly approximate picture of the changes can be made from your evening or morning newspaper alone. If vertical charts are kept showing opening, day's range, and closing prices, a one point chart may be compiled from them. Such computation cannot, of course, show the intermediate changes during the day, but--the result would be fairly approximate.

In the latter connection, a little study is needed. If the full last figure on one point was 55 for example, with the close at 55½, an opening of 56, or better with high 57 plus and close 55 or lower, would call for these added figures, 56, 57, 55. Suppose the next day this stock opens up at 57, or better, rises to 60, or better and closes at 55 7/8, added figures would be 56, 57, 58, 59, 60 and 59. There would probably be intermediate full figure fluctuations between 57-60, and even repetitions of 59 or 58 before the last 59 was reached. However, the picture is approximate. It is the best we can do from a newspaper.

For stocks which do not fluctuate very violently, that are heavily capitalized, and whose full figure fluctuations are not material, the newspaper data, used as described, is a fair substitute plan, but it is by no means accurate or reliable.

It must be distinctly understood that newspaper reports, oftimes hastily compiled, are not intended for close accurate charting purposes. They have not been satisfactory to the author, nor to any conscientious student of this Method. The newspapers themselves usually carry the "waiver clause" in their financial pages, disclaiming responsibility for error.

The tape is the only accurate record.

Anything worth doing at all is worth doing well, particularly when your capital may be involved. It is suggested that the essential figures be obtained from those best qualified to furnish them and who guarantee that they are compiled directly from the tape.

*Such a list of actual full figure changes, in compact, understandable form, is obtainable.   Reliable organizations are qualified to select the best 50 to 100 active stocks, and supply the exact and full figure movements.   These organizations are also in a position to make substitutions where there are indications of new activity, new leaders, and, conversely, where inactivity begins to nullify the value of older figures.

In addition, changes in averages are also important particularly in the Dow-Jones hourly figures, printed on the news tickers.   We also refer herein, page 51, to the special Dow-Jones half-hourly industrial log. It has a particular significance, due to its half point recorded movements, a valuable, close and powerful analytical study in itself.

Proper data should be obtained, and the habit formed of recording same daily.   No real progress can be expected, nor can this Method be fully taken advantage of without proper accessories, the actual records of movements, some of them seemingly trifling, but in reality forming the under-current which finally directs the trend one way or the other.

ELABORATION AND APPLICATION OF DATA

At the slight risk of repetition and for the sake of being more definite, so as to give the student a proper start, we elaborate somewhat on the data and purpose of each set of points, figures, outlines and geometrical outline or practice charts.

The one point charts, the use and method of compiling which already have been explained, should include 50 to 100 stocks, and some good averages.   They can be compiled by the 5, 0 and X system, or the old figure system.   Personal preference must be your guide.

The three point charts are used to summarize the moves of the one points.   They show clearly the worth while intermediate trend swings. They are a condensation that eliminates minor fluctuations.

The five points condense broad moves, and simplify interpretation of wide moving stocks, those advancing or declining 30 to 50 points in a single intermediate semi-cycle.   These can hardly be interpreted satisfactorily in any other way.   These charts indicate the main, long trend.   They condense the time factor and show long term accumulation and distribution.

We also use the *three* and *five* points to interpret the broad moves of the averages, and the market as a whole.

TREND OUTLINE AND GEOMETRICAL CHARTS

Most useful data and a great help to students in the initial phases of learning this Method will be found by keeping trend outlines and the ingenious geometrical - flat top and bottom - charts, see Figure 4. They make for checking, easy reading and more assured interpretations. *Ultimately these aids can be dispensed with.* Use them for a year or less until the points and figures alone will be found sufficient. The author assures you, as facility is gained, the mechanics and work are rewarded by increased fluency in reading, and improved judgment in interpretations.

The trend outline charts are made by merely joining tops and bottoms of moves - the extremes, - of course.   This is different from a vertical line chart, as it is angular, like a series of triangles - without the bases.   The N. Y. Times 5 point page 62, inset, is a sample of a 5 point main trend summary.

The student may dispense with the trend outlines within a few weeks or immediately if the point and figure charts are found sufficient. However, they are desirable, especially for judging the longer and wider swings.   It is possible to compile these in outline, *right on the Point and Figure charts,* in colored pencil or ink.   Sophisticated traders may object to these precautions on the grounds that this suggestion is too simple or elementary.   However, we learned how to read points and figures clearly by outlining the major moves by such trend ortlines.

The stocks to be charted can range from a few to many.   The number must depend on the time available and your inclination.   It does not take long to keep 25, 50, or even 100 stocks.   With the figures provided for the student, their insertion in the charts, is a matter of minutes.

Stocks to be carefully watched are naturally the foremost leaders. While opinions differ on these, we personally watch closely the action of the following:

American Telephone	Union Pacific	U. S. Steel
Consolidated Gas	Atchison	Case Threshing
American Tobacco B	American Can	Allied Chemical
Dupont	Auburn	Air Reduction
N. Y. Central	Sears-Roebuck	Standard Oil N. J.

Any man or any group of men compiling a list of leaders would probably compile a different list, would take issue on the inclusion of some of these, and add others.   However, this broad group going up or down will influence the market accordingly.   As averages they would make up into a good barometric index, we believe.   They include investment issues as well as speculative ones.   Conditions may later warrant changing this list.   For the present, they satisfy us.   Their action is all we need know in order to judge the condition of the market as a whole at the present time.

As, when and if some of the old-line leaders like American Smelting, American Sugar, Anaconda, Montgomery-Ward and similar issues become stabilized at higher levels, so that price disparities will no longer become an objectionable factor, it will be necessary to include them, or substitute some of the more volatile issues now included among the leaders for more stable issues among the stocks apparently graduating into a higher priced class like the foregoing.

THE FIVE ACTIVE LEADERS

Those who watch the tape, and desire to use this Method for trading purposes will find it desirable to compare the fluctuations of the Dow-Jones hourly Industrials, with their personal averages of five active leading stocks, both reduced to points and figures. It is a simple matter to do this work in a few moments, and its resultant picture serves as a check upon other aids to your judgment.

THE RUNNING ACTION LINE

An important technical aid to judging the short swings of the market is the running action line. The preparation and use of a point and figure running action line will be more fully described and explained in our next book.

VIII. MAKING A PRACTICAL START

The underlying thought back of this work is to give you a practical plan or method which will enable you to observe developing phenomena in stock price movements. Once these phenomena are understood, it will be a relatively simple matter for you to develop sufficient skill to analyze them for the purpose of aiding your judgment. This book could be written with greater elaboration or with closer condensation. We have tried to follow a middle course. There is a great danger in relying exclusively upon any one conclusion and we feel it our duty to warn you accordingly. It is not possible merely to read a technical work of this nature and believe it to be a short cut to affluence.

The Method and principles outlined herein, if carefully studied and understood, will permit you to plan your market operations in an orderly and methodical fashion. All will concede that there will be greater probability for profit under this plan, than if you would continue your investing or trading haphazardly. Facility and skill will come after reasonable study and practice. In the arts, sciences and crafts the finished master arrives at his goal, only after considerable preparation. In all the arts and crafts, the student must practice endlessly before attempting to tackle the final work which will brand him as a master. No one method for trading and investing can be evaluated, which will produce consistent profit, unless effort and application is put into a thorough mastery of the technicalities involved. Once you understand the principles we have endeavored to explain, there will be no difficulty in recognizing formations which will repeat themselves constantly, thus enabling you to realize profits.

First master the theory and then proceed with the practical application of it.

In the beginning, it is entirely unnecessary to keep a mass of data and material. A modest start will be ample. The data you decide upon should be kept accurately and neatly. It is better to make records on a few charts and do it well. Begin with a few leading stocks, say approximately 25. Plot them first by one point moves, then by three and finally by five points. Reproduce some of them by geometric figures similar to the plan shown in Figure 4, on page 37. Study the formations as they develop in both types of charts. Include in your group at least ten of the leading issues and the following market averages, either the Herald-Tribune 100 stocks preferred by your author or the Standard Statistics 90 stocks and in addition the three Dow-Jones Indices—30 Industrials—20 Rails—20 Utilities. Do not burden yourself at the beginning with too much work. Master thoroughly the Method, and later, when you develop skill you will be able with but very little effort each day to carry a greater number of different issues, plotted by the one point Method.

Let us start by examining the one point chart of U. S. Steel, Figure 3, which will be found on page 35. There we have prepared

for you the actual data on the movement of this important industrial
issue from the first full point change in the month of March 1933 up to
the date of closing these forms.   After you understand the Method of
preparing the one point chart, as illustrated, proceed to study the
geometrical chart prepared from the same data which is illustrated for
you in Figure 4, on page 37.   A thorough knowledge of these principles should be acquired before proceeding to the three and five point
condensation charts, which are necessary for use in connection with
more volatile issues or of the broader moves.

COMMENCE AT A LOGICAL POINT

It is possible to start your chart anywhere in the movement of a
stock and on any day. It is more desirable, however, to commence at a
logical point.   A logical point to start any chart would be at the top
of the last rally or at the bottom of the last decline. This means, either
where the stock or the market has made a top or where the important support point has caused a reversal of the last intermediate trend.   Any
formation of importance is where a new floor, base or ceiling, or
resistance point is made.   You will soon be able to recognize and
name the type of formation as it occurs, or when it is completed. A
very good point to begin at would be at the *low point* of the bear market
July 1932.   However, it is not necessary to start as far back as that.
An excellent point for beginning your charts is the bottom lows of early
March 1933.   It would be well to obtain a binder of historical data for
the purpose of the study.   The author is trying to influence the publisher to produce such a binder of charts for the aid and assistance of
those who desire to study carefully the different types of formations.

In addition to the one point and geometric graphs, we have reproduced for you our regular three point working sheets Figure 5a, and
five point sheet Figure 5b.   These will be found on page 38.

Your author uses white work sheets for one point , buff sheets for
the three points , and blue sheets for his five points . You will
soon become skilled in reading your geometric charts, at which time
they may be readily dispensed with. In the beginning, however, it would
be well to draw and practice making them.

FIVE POINT MAY BE DEFERRED

For the beginner we do not insist that five point charts be kept.
The five points are a refinement of the Method and will be used for
analyzing the longer main trend and for. catching the moves in the more
volatile issues. Such stocks as Case Threshing, Auburn, Allied Chemical,
International Business Machine, Air Reduction or American Telephone,
when they fluctuate in broad moves must be plotted by the five point
plan in order to recognize formations representing periods of accumulation and distribution.   This Method, either by use of the one point
plan--the three point plan---or the five point plan--will provide a
means for you to ferret out and catch for the purpose of profit all moves
either up or down in any stock.

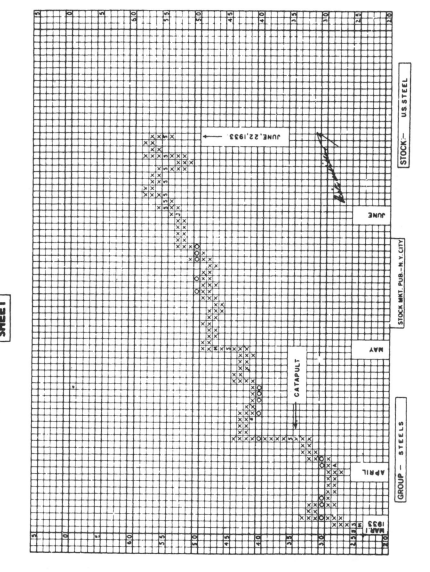

FIGURE - 3

NO. 5001 - ONE POINT

IDEAL
CHARTING
SHEET

STOCK MARKET PUBLICATIONS   NEW YORK CITY

The work of keeping the five point charts is negligible, but certainly most interesting. A five point chart is illustrated and described in Figure 53, on page 38.

U. S. STEEL IN FULL FIGURE ACTION
MARCH 1st, 1933 TO DATE

Here we reproduce the full figure changes of U. S. Steel common compiled from our records of daily price changes. They are the full figure variations omitting, of course, all of the fractions disregarded under this Method. From the figures *given below*, the charts on the following pages have been prepared. You will note that the first full figure change in a new month is entered by use of the first initial of the month instead of by the conventional X, 0 or 5 as would be in ordinary practice. Therefore, the letter M appearing in the square stands for March and 25, A for April and 28, M for May and 49, J for June and 53. The initial letter of the month is not inserted until a full figure change actually occurs, and it represents the first full figure change or any change occurring on the 1st, 2d or 3d or any other day of the new month. Observe below the condensed style of noting the data for the purpose of producing the charts used by this Method. In the line of figures for the month of March, you will notice after the fourth figure we record 32 after the 7. This indicates a straight rise from 27 to 32 either by a movement through the figure or by a gap opening. Gaps are ignored by the Method. See discussion of gaps in Chapter V, page 24. The tenth figure indicates a decline from 31 to 29. Advances or declines beyond the following 10s are noted herein in full, in order to indicate the change. By following each of the figures above and checking them against the U. S. Steel one point graph the progression of the movement as well as the plan of recording both charts and moves will be clearly understood. Once you have this full figure change data it is a very simple matter to prepare these graphs. Further and detailed instructions will be found in Chapter V, page 22.

	M
March	25, 4, 8, 7, 32, 3, 1, 2, 1, 29, 8, 30, 29, 8, 9, 8, 9, 8, 9, 7,

	A
April	28, 9, 30, 29, 30, 2, 1, 3, 2, 3, 2, 4, 8, 44, 2, 3, 2, 3, 2,
	3, 2, 0, 2, 0, 1, 0, 1, 0, 2, 4, 3, 4, 3, 23, 3, 2, 3, 2, 1, 3, 6.

	M
May	49, 8, 9, 8, 7, 8, 7, 9, 7, 8, 6, 7, 6, 9, 8, 9, 50, 49, 8, 7,
	8, 9, 50, 49, 8, 7, 9, 51, 49, 51, 3, 2, 3, 2.

	J
June	53, 4, 2, 3, 2, 3, 4, 3, 4, 6, 5, 6, 4, 5, 6, 8, 7, 8, 7, 5, 7,
	6, 2, 3, 1, 3, 7, 8, 6, 7.

After thoroughly understanding the preparation of the one point graphs, and the conventional one point geometric charts, it would be well for you to draw a few trend outlines superimposed upon your one point pictures. Trend outlines are drawn from the high to the low point and from the low to the high point of each succeeding rally as it occurs.

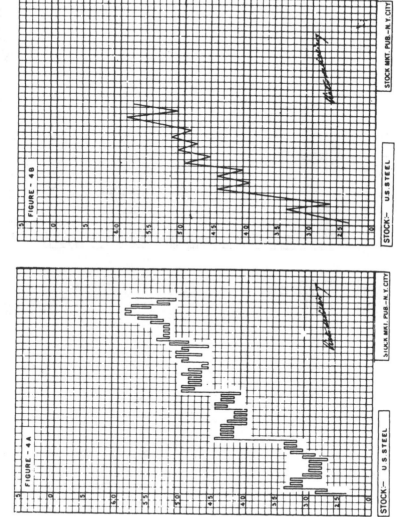

ONE POINT MOVES
GEOMETRICAL

FIGURE - 4A

STOCK:— U S STEEL

STOCK MKT. PUB.—N.Y.CITY

ONE POINT MOVES
TREND OUTLINE

FIGURE - 4 B

STOCK:— U.S. STEEL

STOCK MKT. PUB.—N.Y.CITY

38

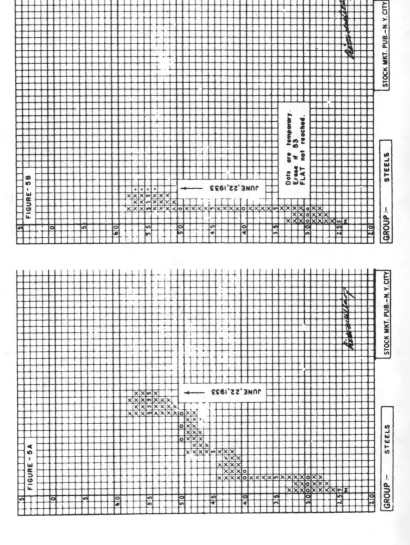

U.S. STEEL
(5 POINT)

FIGURE - 5B

JUNE. 22, 1933

Dots are temporary.
Erase if 53
FLAT not reached.

GROUP :— STEELS

STOCK MKT. PUB.—N.Y. CITY

U.S. STEEL
(3 POINT)

FIGURE - 5A

JUNE. 22, 1933

GROUP :— STEELS

STOCK MKT. PUB.—N.Y. CITY

 IDEAL CHARTING SHEET

IX.   IMPORTANT GUIDES TO THE USE OF THE METHOD

In order to use this Method as a guide in your market transactions, the following important rules should be thoroughly studied and faithfully observed.   To ignore them will be a distinct handicap.

I.   *DIVERSIFICATION:* Commitments should be spread out moderately, as far as possible, by buying or selling equal quantities of stock in several companies.   Instead of trading in 100 share lots of a single issue, buy or sell 25 shares each of four different issues.   Study the characteristics of a group of at least 25 stocks, so that you will know their pecularities.   Do not concentrate in any one issue.   Do not hold one stock because you believe it is a good one, nor sell another because you believe it is a bad one.   Bad stocks go up and good ones go down. Statistics and news are the basis for trading and investing are factors which belong to rules of years gone by.   Today is a new day, a new deal for every stock.   Therefore, spread out your commitments, for in so doing you minimize your risk and better your chances for profit.

II.   *AWAIT CULMINATIONS:* The market is always here.   Every advance will reach its culmination, it will come to rest and reverse itself eventually.   The same holds true of a decline.   Sooner or later, either a ceiling or a floor is formed on your charts.   Wait for these important formations.   They form the most favorable points for buying or for selling, for establishing a long position, or for going short.   In this connection long bases, long periods of accumulation, furnish the best opportunities for intermediate swing investments.   This is especially true when these formations develop in the three and five point charts. If the work, backing and filling in a trading area, appears to be a new floor, the longer the base continues, the more stock is being accumulated by the insiders, and the more stock accumulated the more substantial the support and more aggressive the advance.   Where these formations try your patience, it will be profitable for you not to be impulsive.

III.   *ALWAYS UNDERTRADE:* It is always better to undertrade than to overtrade.   This is the one great secret of success and will lead if followed to consistent profit.   Never buy for investment after the market has had a rapid and sharp advance. Avoid thinly margined commitments. A margin call is a sign that your judgment has proven wrong.   Stop orders should be spread out to correct all errors.   By understanding and the intelligent use of this Method, you will avoid getting margin calls.   Place your commitments with the moving active stocks.   It is unwise to take positions prematurely.   Do not tie up your capital before the major interests have created the base.   When they get ready to move the stock, then it is time enough for you to place your commitments.   One of the most advantageous positions to buy is at the catapult.   It is always better to join forces with the active groups of investors and traders. Go along with them while they are moving.   Get out when they start distributing.   Remember stock sponsors and pools will force their issues just so far and no further.   When active market interests move their stocks, go with them. When they switch to other issues, switch with them. Never trade in sympathy stocks. They will be reached in time.   Go with the leaders.

IV. *TAKE ADVANTAGE OF GROUP ACTION:* Stocks move in groups. It is well to watch the trends in the broad groups. All groups do not go up at one time. Conversely, all groups do not go down at the same time. While it is true that the market usually moves in unison, you will find that strong groups decline less than the market and advance more, and weak groups will advance less than the market and decline more. Watch your group action. Use your capital by participating in group action when it occurs.

V. *AVERAGING DOWN:* This practice caused many of the bear market losses. While it is dangerous to average a long position in a bear market, averaging may be used advantageously on long positions in a bull market. Careless, irrational averaging can become disastrous. However, if you average in harmony with the movement and with the trend of the market and your purchases are made at favorable spots, averaging can prove very profitable. After a stubborn base has been formed, subsequent to a reasonable decline, a sound place to make your second purchase is at that point, with the second commitment protected with stop orders under the immediate proceeding work or trading range.

VI. *PYRAMIDING:* Pyramiding is a rather confusing term and really means averaging up. It means go with the main trend upward and buy further lots, as and when new ceilings have been completed, and are at the point of being left behind, where they will then become potential new floors. When such formations have been completed, further lots may be purchased but should be protected with suitable stop orders placed beneath the work. This procedure can also be used advantageously by the investor. The proper place for pyramiding on intermediate swing investments is to purchase additional commitments after the sharp advances have been corrected and when the corrections show support formations, buy after the support begins to reveal itself. Pyramiding is not as dangerous as some would have us believe, provided, however, it is done intelligently and with the use of stop orders properly placed.

VII. *ANTICIPATING THE EXTENT OF THE MARKET:* Some technicians are of the opinion that the Method will persistently foretell the extent of subsequent rallies or declines. It is claimed that the length of the work--ceiling or floor--can be used for the purpose of estimating the probable future action, either up or down. Your author, in his many years of careful research, has not found any one principle to be sufficiently dependable. You will be able, from your observation and study, to recognize those types of patterns which prove to have forecasting qualities. Do not demand too much of this Method. It is a valuable aid to your judgment. Use it as such.

X. MOST PROFITABLE OPPORTUNITIES REVEALED BY THIS METHOD

To follow the market intelligently, the course of the leaders must be watched and carefully charted. All will admit they lead the market. We deem it advisable to caution the student not to play his favorites and ignore the balance of the market which the entire world is watching. Concentrating on your favorite or pet stock may cause you to miss the important moves in others, which are considered by the major interests, as leaders in the current market. Any stock, group of stocks, any published index or privately compiled index, any commodity or group of commodities, may be charted and analyzed by the Point and Figure Method.

It is a safe and conservative statement for us to make when we state, no stock or group of stocks, no commodity or group of commodities will fail to form patterns from which you can easily select profitable positions for trading and investing. The basis upon which this Method relies is supply and demand. Support and subsequent demand for stock promptly register easily recognizable formations on your graphs. Supply and subsequent pressure, is similarly recognizable when they form ceilings on your graphs. Therefore, in the beginning, without regard for your personal preference, plot the real leaders by this Method. You will soon become skilled in recognizing indications of supply and demand. When this has occurred, you can very easily extend yourself and soon you will be able to keep a close watch on 100 or more active and inactive stocks. For general convenience keep all charts in alphabetical order. Some organizations keep them in groups. Either method is satisfactory. For the average person, the alphabetical is considered best by your author. Newspapers list stocks in alphabetical arrangement and the full figure data is published alphabetically.

If you keep your stocks alphabetically, it will save much time in compiling your records. It is well to mark each of your charts, both with the name of the stock it represents and the group into which the stock is classified. It is true that even a limited number of stocks faithfully kept and recorded, will furnish a guide to the probable price path movement of that particular handful, but, it is a handicap to be without the guidance of the market as a whole. It must be noted that a sufficient number of stocks must be tabulated in order to get an harmonious idea of the market as a whole.

Elsewhere, we have already written of leadership, and the stocks which at present comprise that group. However, leadership shifts from time to time. This is a matter which the student will recognize as time goes on.

Do not hesitate to be flexible--to substitute new leaders or new opportunities, as they make their appearance. In recent months good illustrations have been available which show the importance of flexibility. Be flexible. Follow the new leaders as they develop.

We had a period of interesting railroad stock price movements with no pronounced leadership in any particular group. With the advent of discussions anent the repeal of the Eighteenth Amendment to the Constitution, interest centered around the stocks to be benefited by abandonment of Prohibition. Some of these securities became real leaders and furnished good opportunities. We might not have been willing to be guided by their implications as affecting the market as a whole, but the market is always *up-to-date*. It is always modernizing itself, and to be reactionary as to trends and fashions, if we can call it that, is to miss some amazing opportunities.

It is to be noted that every participant in the stock market is there because of financial reasons or mercenary purposes of some kind. He is there to make money, or to invest favorably in equities which will produce money for him--profit.

THE EFFECT OF INFLATION ON EQUITIES

Great opportunities came along with the advent of "The New Deal," the abandonment of our Gold Standard, and the admitted Administration Policy of controlled inflation, with 1926 average prices as an object- ive. This placed a premium on new possibilities. It placed a premium on commodity stocks, with variable equities in inventory stocks, metal stocks and such others as would be influenced by a policy tending to inflate the price level.

THE SECONDARY ISSUES

When we speak about leaders, one may ask "What are leaders?" The answer is, they are stocks of any name or description which *lead* or in- fluence the market.

Watch and observe therefore the leaders, new or old, with an open mind as to your selection, and see whether or not you care to trade or invest in any or all of them. Keep them for the record. They will come in handy at some future time.

All issues, excepting the leaders, are secondary to the leaders in their action and, therefore, are properly designated, as secondary issues. However, in this class, during a period of recovery from a major bear market, very many of the former leading stocks become moder- ately priced and no longer lead the market, and because of their large floating supply, popularity and public appeal they are secondary in importance to the leaders. In this class we may well include such stocks as New York Central, Delaware Lackawanna & Western, Pennsylvania American Smelting and Refining, American Sugar Refining, and stocks of similar descriptions which formerly stood high in the averages and price, and their investment possibilities highly regarded. The investor and trader now has a chance to participate in their movements and profitable trading opportunities, with a minimum of risk, and no significant capi- tal requirement as was formerly necessary.

The third group to be noted are what might be considered trailers. Some of the trailers are former high priced issues, some in the seasoned investment class, some moderately priced. They furnish many good oppor- tunities when active, and are considered trailers only when they have lost their speculative following.

The so-called specialty stocks, with lower capitalization and rather erratic movements, depending upon special influences, are parti- cularly amenable to diagnosis by the Point and Figure Method. We claim, based upon experience, that no one, proficient in this Method, need now fear the difficulty of investing or trading in specialties. By keeping their moves charted by one and three points conscientiously, the main movements in them will show up clearly, and furnish a maximum of insur- ance at a minimum of real risk.

THE LOW PRICED STOCKS

As to the lower priced stocks, these also are highly susceptible to diagnosis by this Method. However, there are many technical considerations involved in the action of low priced stocks. They furnish opportunities for unusual profits, quite disproportionate to the risk assumed.* This group is in a class by itself. Mere low price cannot defy the ability of this Method to analyze their moves. By all means study low priced stocks. Chart them on the one and three point graphs.

XI   HOW TO RECOGNIZE UNUSUAL OPPORTUNITIES FOR PROFIT

It is largely by the Point and Figure Method that one is able to take advantage of unusual opportunities. Both the actual turning points as well as other points in new moves, are clearly indicated by this Method. We whole-heartedly and unqualifiedly endorse this Method, because of the logical recording of the important changes in the movement of stocks, coupled with the practical bird's-eye view of the periods during which stocks are prepared for important moves, both up and down. Also because of the exclusive way in which this Method presents a clear picture of past performances, together with the scientific basis upon which conclusions may be reached.

We have mentioned the terms 'catapult and semi-catapult' as the logical and vital places where positions should be adopted. This has proven itself over and over again. While these points do not invariably develop to be absolutely certain in their implications as to each and every stock, each and every time they are developed, the percentage of probability for profit at these points is far in excess of the probability for loss. To take a position at such a time is therefore wise for it will invariably prove to be more profitable than unprofitable. Always remember that the only risk a real trader should take is a small loss which would be occasioned by the execution of a stop order wisely placed.

THE CATAPULT

We can confidently state that when the catapult formation is reached, that point is probably the beginning of an opportunity to take a position on a really scientific basis. A cursory examination of the graph on page 44, will disclose a form very familiar to students of physics. The dictionary defines a catapult as, an ancient military engine for hurling missiles. The catapult hurls missiles by sudden force which is sufficient to temporarily upset the law of gravity. The fine balance of this force is on the fulcrum. An exact parallel is to be found in the action of stocks when plotted by this Method. When demand overcomes supply in the fulcrum and stocks get out on the catapult a good move is more than a probability. The reason a stock should

*See "Low Priced Stocks—How and When to Buy Them" by Owen Taylor, Stock Market Publications.

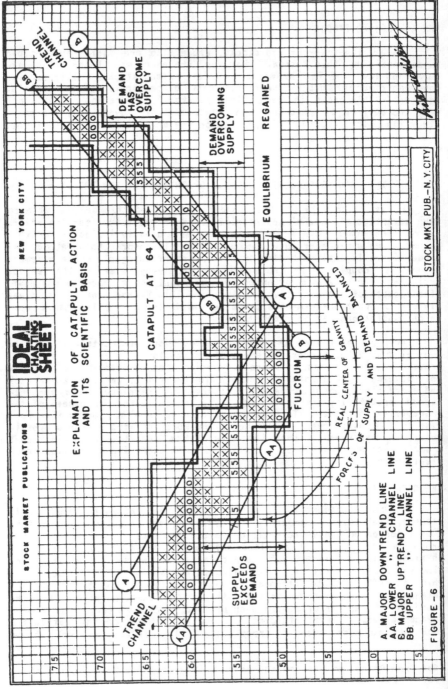

FIGURE – 6

scientifically and logically proceed upward, as if hurled from a force under and behind it, is best explained by the diagram we have prepared so as to make it clear.

In the down trend channel between the lines A and AA, supply exceeds demand.   There you will find a clearly defined downward path, lower tops, lower bottoms, a clear trend channel heading downward. There is no indication where demand will overcome supply or where the trend will turn.   It is unnecessary to guess or to take chances when using this Method.   Stocks have a bottom. The bottom will come when demand overcomes supply.   You will be able to easily recognize this situation when it develops.

CONJECTURE IS NOT FOUNDATION OF UNDERLYING PRINCIPLES

Refer to graph Figure 6 , page 44, from 63 top to first 50, we do not know as yet whether the decline will cease, or whether it will have really started at 50. The 50 line spreads. Then, 51, 52 and 53 each get longer. Is this going to be a new ceiling or another "floor"? At 53 the rise goes through the down trend line A. At 55 we have a rather promising looking ladle-shaped picture, suggesting that major interests have scooped up everything from 50 to 53.   Trend channel is changed here to an upward tilt, and at 57 there is no doubt the former bearish picture is altered completely. Is it a false move? Let the conservatives wait for further developments.

The centre of gravity thus far, is around the fourth or fifth 50 figure.   On decline to 53 long lines begin to form at that point namely five 53s thence nine 54s and then eight 55s.   Previously there were seven 55s.   The picture as a whole suggests that equilibrium has been clearly regained.   At 60 demand is increased and at 58 we are given an opportunity of studying the real trend.   We can now plot a tentative main trend and trend channel line, see lines B and BB.   The heavy outlines sketched in to bring out the picture sharply need not be made. We have drawn them in to illustrate how the student should visualize each and every picture, so that real training is had.   Visualizing in this manner will develop your judgment and will ultimately replace the mechanics of tracing in these lines.   At 64 the catapult is developed and at 65 a new stage of the move is plotted.

We always regard the 5 and 10 points as something new in the life of the movement of a stock. *The public thinks that way.*   The major operators are also well aware of the fact that the public thinks that way, hence it pays to go along with them.   This illustration clearly shows the development of the full and complete catapult theory.   When no previous formation showing the forces of supply and demand balancing each other is at hand, the student should endeavor to ascertain the broad previous moves, because full and sufficient catapult position may exist. Take advantage of the opportunity to study previous weeks or months of prior moves.

Movements by three point stages with subsequent catapult formations arc even more convincing and profitable than are the conclusions drawn from the one points alone. The risk is no greater than when taking a position when a catapult is indicated on the three point chart. The possibility of profit is proportionately enhanced especially in broad and intermediate swing moves. We have submitted herewith the scientific basis upon which the catapult theory is based and it is presented as a logical study of the force of supply and demand--a phenomena in physics, that rests firmly on a scientific foundation.

THE SEMI-CATAPULT

A semi-catapult formation also offers some opportunity for profit. In this formation the balance of force is not as clearly defined as in the full catapult. In the formation known as the semi-catapult we might not have a perfect fulcrum, nor the much sought for formation, described by this author as a ladle, the handle being the A and AA channel, the base at the fulcrum and the lip of the ladle at the point of completion, namely 55-57 in our illustration.

A semi-catapult can also develop above the work at depression point where a new high price is made. It is difficult to recognize a semi-catapult in this position. One may follow the semi-catapult formation with reasonable assurances for profit. However, always use a stop order to protect your commitments.

XII.   ANALYZE THE TECHNICAL POSITION BY OBSERVING FORMATIONS

It is most instructive to study the contours and formations of your Point and Figure charts in order to familiarize yourself with their various characteristics. This advice applies equally to the one, three and five points. It also applies to individual stocks as well as to the averages.

Stocks have habits just like human beings. Certain stocks in similar groups take their cue from or attempt to duplicate the rough outline of their leaders. This is not an iron-clad rule, but it is well to observe which stocks lead and which follow. This with a view of profiting from subsequent moves where the same habit will be followed. This habit develops too often to be considered a mere coincidence or accident.

Then again, stocks ordinarily regarded as staid may develop volatile tendencies at any time. Watch for these symptoms. Take nothing for granted. On the other hand a stock ordinarily regarded as volatile, a fast mover, may remain inactive or disappoint the anticipated broad move by inactivity or narrow range. This may take place particularly during a longer period of accumulation, or distribution. Observe what happens after it gets out of the then current trading area--or accumulation or distribution. Such area nearly always represents the former or the latter. It is not usually the habit of volatile stocks to remain inactive for a long period of time. By watchful waiting, recording and observing, splendid moves with good profits will be the reward.

STRONG AND WEAK TECHNICAL POSITIONS

The technical position of a stock or the market is strong when demand exceeds supply.   It is weak when supply exceeds demand.   The technical position is very strong after a period of accumulation following a major decline.   It is very weak after a period of distribution following a major rise.

The one points should, in the case of a strong technical position show an extended line of work with either a well-formed fairly solid base, or a series of bases like a descending stairway.   The bottom step is preferably longer than the preceding majority.   The base may he irregular, or broken into a series of bases.   In the latter case the three points give a consolidated clearer picture, and may tell the story more quickly.

Conversely, a weak technical position, is often revealed after a series of advances which, by one point charting, reveal a series of higher levels, like an ascending stairway.   The rise is not usually halted by mere technical advances, declines or flurries.   The picture as a whole should be your guide.   The time arrives when the advances are neither as vigorous nor as confident.   The ascending stairway pattern begins to give way to a series of confused and halting movements. This is due to the churning motion around the tops which you will soon recognize as distribution.   It is due to the conflict between the bulls and bears--supply overcoming demand.   It is important at this stage to check against the three points, in order to observe consolidated moves, and to judge whether or not a real ceiling has been formed temporarily. By some technicians, the temporary distributive formation is described as a congestion point, and we think it is an admirable term.

DETERMINING INTERMEDIATE MOVES.

It has been wisely said by able operators and skilled tape readers, "give them room to fluctuate."   It is the habit of stocks to fluctuate. The investor or trader must allow for advances and declines in reasonable proportion to the prior movement.   If the movement has been a broad one, allow for corresponding broader technical advances or declines. Normally, the major wide moving stocks may advance or decline 10, 15 or 20 points without altering the intermediate or main trend.   We admit this is an arbitrary yardstick reckoned in points.   A better idea is gained by past performances in individual stocks, by studying the former trend outlines and estimating or anticipating the extent of the next move, from the three point charts.

In the slower, lower priced issues a 7 to 10 point move is accounted sufficient to correct the technical position either way, without affecting the intermediate or main trend. This is, likewise, not a yardstick but an approximation.

Ordinarily, in higher priced issues, a 5 point correction is strictly normal while in the lower priced division, a 3 point correction is also regarded as normal.   However, such corrections must happen within the average price zone, and neither materially above congestion points new highs or on the catapult, nor below the clear levels of support and resistance.

SOLID FORMATIONS GIVE CONFIDENCE

We like to see a fairly solid advance, each stage well consolidated before the next stage is being reached, with only normal technical reactions intervening.   The formation during declines should be equally confident.   If the formations are broken, ragged, confusing, the indications suggest caution.   It is an indication of conflict and indecision.   Such formations during a major advance give rise to air pockets under the congestion points, in the form of ellipses, semi-circles or irregular arcs.   We speak elsewhere of this type of formation as an arched ellipse.   Such formations usually are advance warnings of a major change of trend forthcoming.   Watch your three points for these indications.

XIII.   GAUGING THE LENGTH AND CULMINATION OF MOVES

Attempts have been made and aids invented for the purpose of using this Method in determining the extent of the probable future moves, either up or down.   It would be an ideal situation were we able to use the past work as a mechanical means of judging future movements.   Does this Method answer the question asked by most traders and investors, namely, "How far up or how far down will the next move go?" The Method itself furnishes the best clues and your experience together with your judgment, as it develops, will show you where and when a move is likely to terminate. It is impossible to reduce this to a matter of a formula.   We have already intimated that the market is not to be conquered by a system nor can we reduce it to a problem of button pushing.   Nothing can ever replace the skill and judgment which comes with practice and experience. Certain technicians have represented that the so-called count system will forecast the extent of a move.   The count system relies upon the number of times certain full figures register during a trading range—work area.   In our opinion any plan that would reduce stock market action to a formula must fail.   It must be wrong as many times as it is right and therefore in the long run nullifies itself.   In the humble opinion of your author, many plans which can be used for this purpose that cannot be relied upon and be correct eight out of ten times must be discarded.

We prefer to depend upon the composite results furnished by the three point consolidated picture and the double tops and bottom indicated on the one point charts.   The three point consolidation throws into discard all minor full figure fluctuations caused by daily trading and gives a more dependable summary where the foundation--base or the congestion area--ceiling is to be found.   From the composite of both charts and a broader survey of each, your judgment will be the best guide as to what will happen.

A broad three point base should be followed by a substantial advance.   Conversely, a solid three point congestion area should have a corresponding,* equal and opposite decline.   While this rule is not absolutely reliable at all times, it works out in a great majority of cases.* Action and re-action in physics are usually equal.   This is also a normal phenomena of price movements.

*Similar to Newton's Law.

With reference to anticipation of the termination or culmination of an intermediate market, we have preferred to reply upon formations known as double tops and double bottoms whether complete or partial, for deduction of the termination of the move. It is useless to try to determine the exact top or bottom within fractions. The Method will guide you to take the meat out of each move. Congestion points at the top or bottom will give you the signal to take your profits. After a major advance or decline the plottings on the three point charts furnish an excellent guide from which you will see the end of the move. It is reasonable to expect a 1/3 to a 1/2 advance or decline correcting the previous move. As you develop skill you will soon be able to recognize whether a correction is a normal one or whether it is but the beginning of a major move in the opposite direction.

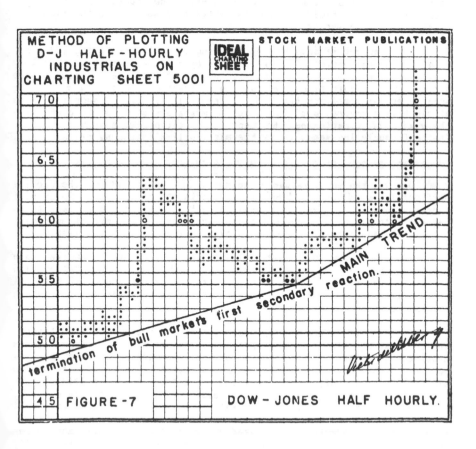

METHOD OF PLOTTING D-J HALF-HOURLY INDUSTRIALS ON CHARTING SHEET 5001

STOCK MARKET PUBLICATIONS

FIGURE-7   DOW - JONES HALF HOURLY.

XIV.   CONSOLIDATING YOUR WORK THROUGH THE AVERAGES

It is vitally important, in our opinion, to number among your charts a few well known, widely followed averages such as the N. Y. Times 50, the Herald-Tribune 100, and the three excellent sets furnished by the Dow-Jones Wall Street Journal, organization. The latter is known everywhere and the averages are furnished in three convenient groups, the 30 Industrials, 20 Rails and 20 Public Utilities.

As to the Industrials, because they are given hourly, a more sensitive one point chart is available. The three and five points can be constructed from the one point data. By having access to the Dow-Jones Industrial hourly figures we have more *work built up in our* one points, a better picture of the price path, the course it took to get there, and a stronger clue to the intricate processes - manipulation - by which such course was arrived at.

A refinement is possible by securing the half-hourly log and plotting same by half points.* This data is by no means essential, but very helpful. Attention is called to it, because of its immense value to the author at difficult times and during confused movements, in a trading area, when the immediate trend is somewhat in doubt. At such times one should have a neutral position. But, if means are at hand for confirming the wisdom of questioning the technical position, we should use them. The half-hourly log seems to be the missing link in the averages.

IMPORTANCE OF DOW-JONES HALF HOURLY LOG CHARTED BY HALF POINTS

One of the most valuable adjuncts of the Method is the special *half point* log of the *half* hourly movements of the Dow-Jones industrial averages that can be kept and compiled by the investor and trader. Keeping such close tabs on a reliable cross-section of the market has many outstanding advantages, not secured by any other form of compilation.

The Dow-Jones 30 Industrial averages are printed and available hourly as already explained. The method of prompt computation and furnishing the figures every thirty minutes, is something our statistical organization worked out. The figures are not accessible to the public but may be secured.

For the immediate trend, short swing, for the board room trader, the computation reduced to an approximate half point chart, from figures supplied indicates every major, minor and intermediate swing of any importance whatever. It builds up a picture of *the tape itself*, as an aid to a trader of only fair ability, it is dependable and helpful and far more reliable than trusting to tape reading. For the more experienced, the Dow-Jones half hourly log in half point form is a formidable tool of his trade that he would not care to dispense with once its value was known. For the investor, interested in the intermediate, main and longer trend, a picture of unrivalled accuracy and dependability is eventually built up. It is of such clearness that he who runs may read.

For your instruction, we have especially compiled such a log from February 27, 1933 to date of going to press. This period has been se-

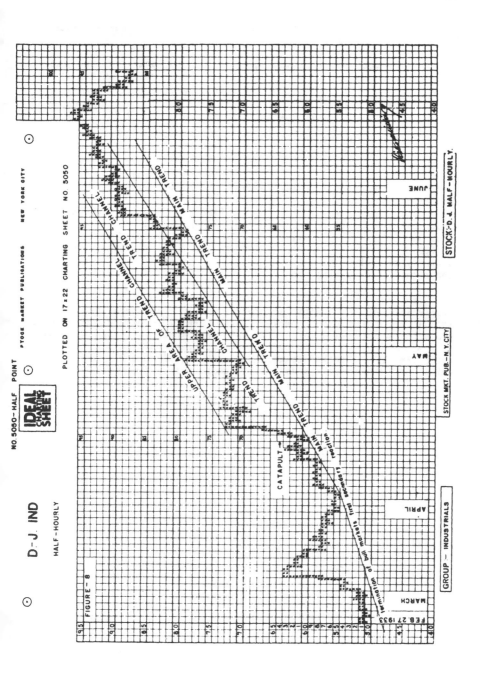

FIGURE - 8

lected because of its difficulty marketwise, and the unusual reversal of
market form since March I.

The procedure for plotting a half point chart follows the same
principles as for any other by this Method. Progression of the *full half*
figure is always to the right, in the nearest available space. However, to
allow ample room and to prevent any confusion, the author uses an en-
larged charting sheet, 17 x 22, medium weight, ruled 4 squares per inch.
Within each square is sufficient space for 4 symbols - an x, 0, or 5. In
other respects the paper is merely an enlargement of the standardized
one point charting paper. Each square provides for two *half* point movements, the base of square being counted the full figure, and space above
plus one half. On the large sheets we use digits and ciphers as in conventional form, placing them, however, on base of square to right or left
as the movement dictates.

By *following* the graphic chart, Figure 8, with me, just a few figures, the simplicity of the procedure will be apparent. The opening fig-
ures are 50$\frac{1}{2}$, 1, 1$\frac{1}{2}$, 1, 1$\frac{1}{2}$, 1, 0$\frac{1}{2}$, 50, 0$\frac{1}{2}$, 1, 0$\frac{1}{2}$, 1, 1$\frac{1}{2}$, 1, 1$\frac{1}{2}$, 1, 1$\frac{1}{2}$,
1, 1$\frac{1}{2}$, 2, 2$\frac{1}{2}$, 2, 1$\frac{1}{2}$, 1, -$\frac{1}{2}$, 1, 1$\frac{1}{2}$, 2, 1$\frac{1}{2}$, 2, 2$\frac{1}{2}$, 3, 3$\frac{1}{2}$, 4, 4$\frac{1}{2}$, 5, 5$\frac{1}{2}$,
etc. By checking the graph against these figures, alone or with a friend,
the method of recording should be clear.

An essential, basic movement like that of the Dow-Jones half
hourly Industrial log deserves your especial consideration, because it
is the whole industrial market. It is hardly possible for any other
group to buck its indicated trend. I recommended a large chart because
of the ease of recording, quick reference, and permanent value. Important organizations prefer to keep basic charts of this type on an office
wall. No. 5050 is really ideal for such purpose. I have personally found
it so.

However, for those who prefer standard size, uniform charts because of their portability, the regular No. 5001 can also be used with
a minimum of eye-strain or confusion by following the reproduced suggestion for keeping them - see Figure 7. We use usual ciphers for full
figures, a heavy dot for the 5 stages and small dots for the half point
figure.

Finally, to avoid errors in plotting half points until facility
and accuracy comes, as it will come in time, let the student treat each
change, half a point of course, as a regular change in the identical manner
that one points are handled, with the single exception that each square
must allow for four symbols.

The formations of the Dow-Jones half hourly log are interesting.
The sharp rise and fall of early March was an unusual one. The initial
13 point move, 50-63$\frac{1}{2}$ could reasonably and technically call for a
halt way reaction, not from presumed base at 50 but from the *logical
jump ng off* place after first strong support above that figure. This
was 51$\frac{1}{2}$, see graph. Rise to be corrected was, therefore half way down
from 51$\frac{1}{2}$-63$\frac{1}{2}$ - 12 points total gain, - 6 points correction. The decline
might have halted at 57$\frac{1}{2}$ which would have been an *average* normal correction. The decline found strong support at 55-55$\frac{1}{2}$. It will be recalled
that conditions at that time fostered investment and trading suspicion

and scepticism. However, when the turn came, it did so decisively according to this log, and never wavered substantially till 97 was reached. This log was on the catapult at 64, and the averages gave a wonderful account of themselves when this point was reached and crossed. An almost straight up 33 point advance in the Dow-Jones Industrial Averages was recorded therefrom.

The clearly defined main uptrend line, and the well formed trend channel between 70 and 95 reminds us forcibly that the stock market does not follow whim or caprice, but a well-defined path that we have only to follow, in order to profit.

XV. POINTS AND FIGURES ARE WEEKS AHEAD OF "TIPS"

Nearly everybody has a general idea of the prestige and investment background of Western Union common $100 par, former dividend $8 with an investment flavor ostensibly sound enough to pass on to one's grand-children. Authorities of an older generation counselled investors to buy and put it away for keeps whenever it was available at bargain prices. Bull market 1929 high was above 270 and bear market low was 12 3/8, 1932. It rallied from the latter figure to around 50, September 1932 and again slumped to a low around 17 during the double bottom of the long bear market, apparently culminating March 1933. This Method, not only indicated the safe bargain price at *which* to buy it, but proved to be the best tip *where* to buy it, and *when* to buy it weeks ahead of what was later to be a 46 point rise from the base, 18 to a temporary congestion area or bullish culmination 64, within less than 10 weeks.

We have compiled a chart of the fluctuations of Western Union from mid-October 1932 to date, according to the Method, by one and three point moves. Figures 9 and 10. Much of the data is self-explanatory.

Reference to the one point chart, Figure 9, shows failure to hold 29-31 zone of mid-October 1932, and first aggressive support at 28-27. Lower resistance at 26 after 5 point drop, warned of sufficient temporary reaction. Double bottom at 26 confirmed this. A 4 point rally to 30 indicated inherent *ability* to rally. A 2 point decline, normal to 28 - new support base, with length of horizontal 28 line indicated improved technical position for time being.   Temporary diagnosis would be "Buy at 29 stop at 26 - old support." Through 30 again, a quick run-up to 36 - 10 points from low, proved ample for time being.   Resistance 34-35 and failure to carry through, added to fact that we have had a 10 point advance warned of a major or minor change shortly. Emphatic drop, 36-35, with a 50° angle on downside, a solid ceiling of resistance at 35, 4 times, 34, 6 times, points to possibility of new base. Stock must snap back sharply from 31, particularly after double bottom there, or we go short on next rally with stop at 37 - to be conservative. At double bottom, 31, another feeble rally, 2 points, to 33, continues the lower bottom. The Method indicates, "sell here - at market." At treble bottom 31 with a stop to limit loss placed at 34 is sufficient. That price, if reached would change the angle, show rallying ability, and

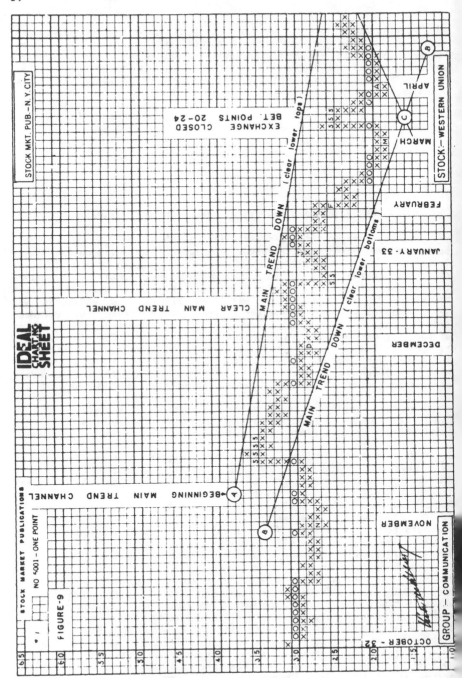

FIGURE-9

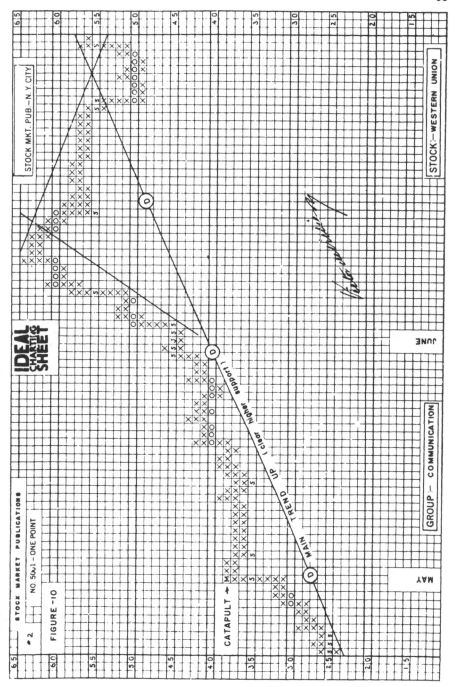

indicate possible run up through the stubborn 35-36 mark.

At 30, down through new base, low for move 27 indicates attempt
at support at same old support levels, 26-27. By now a trend channel
is forming - see lines A and B. We get this by joining or noting
lower tops for time being. At third 26 entire rise is cancelled prov-
ing that move to 36 was false, and not a sustained rise. For whatever
purpose, running in of shorts, distribution of support purchases previously, 26-28, it is recorded that the trend is more likely down than
up. A 4 point rally to 31 proves, plenty of stock for sale around 30. See
great repetition of this figure. As to latter, possible diagnosis could
be, but is not a logical one that there might be accumulation 28-30.
But the bearish formation after 32 is recorded, lower top, with clear
main trend line down, and trend channel dropping in the wrong direction gives indications of a bearish rather than bullish viewpoint. Subsequent decline to 25 is followed by 6 point rally 31, more than enough
to correct possible oversold position. Last rise 31 continues a perfectly
bearish picture, with an excellent opportunity to progress main trend
line just over 36, 32, 31

Throughout January and February while the trend of Western Union
was clearly down, stock was evidently allowed to shift for itself. On
the strength of all previous work, an approximate estimate of around 20
down to 15 could have been made for its bear market final low. Its full
figure was 18, while actual fractional low was 17½. Why do we estimate
20-15? The long liquidation around 30 - probably distress selling rather
than distribution - justified a major shakeout and correction, normally
10-15 points. Therefore, it was time to watch the situation at 20 or below.

The 18 figure is reached in the extremely bearish February - March
1933 markets, a drastic lower bottom, with main downtrend line intact,
and trend channel still clear, forming a bottle-neck cove, with an un-
deniable downward tilt. Rather stubborn resistance at 19 follows   6
times, a nice flat supporting line at 18, 4 times: activity judged
by changes drying up, bank failures, statewide moratoria, bad news, the
N. Y. Stock Exchange about to close, and - Western Union holding the
line at 18. A drop to 15 looks dubious. The Exchange reopens with
a sharp run up in Western Union to 26 continuing lower tops, but, never-
theless stages an 8 point rally under extremely adverse circumstances.
By beginning of April the long base, 19-18 is improving, and although
the entire rise is cancelled temporarily, changes are few, supply is
drying up, the 19 line is drawing out, and a nice bullish upward angle
is forming, 19-25. By continuing our main downtrend line it goes through
around 24 at C. If the stock can go to 27 and hold there, the picture
would alter radically. It does! Merely by joining last 19 to last 25,
and continuing the line in both directions, we get an intersection at C,
where we estimated final low around 15 might be reached and tentative new
main trend line DCD is established.

On the rise to 27, the downward tendency is broken for the first
time in months. No longer do we get a series of new lows. This is a new
high. 27 is also a semi-catapult, just tentative, but in conjunction with
other indications, an extremely bullish spot. The stock refuses to react.
From there it runs into urgent buying and covering at 27-36, recovering all

its loss since mid-November 1932. At this stage note the evident activity of daily full point changes-not volume-from the increasing distance
of verticals of April-May contrasted with December to April inclusive.
At 37, Western Union is on the catapult - a new high for months, then a
drawn out 2-3 point trading range clearly indicating a consolidation of
gains, stubborn buying at 37, double bottom at 35, main uptrend line holding, and market as a whole very confident.

The timid investor or slow trader could have bought Western Union
around 27 with confidence, and surely no hesitation could have been
possible at 37. The long drawn-out work in 35-39 zone might have been
construed as a little distribution, admittedly. But, other indications
mentioned, contradicted such viewpoint. It proved to have been accumulation by the quick rise across 40, aggressive support there, unusual
activity, many changes, and then, the great demonstration or push up
so typical of *temporary* culminations pointed out elsewhere in this book.
This work from around 46 to recent high at 64 fulfills professional
expectations and is strictly - "according to Hoyle." Note the May-June
1933 activity, 30 vertical squares within the month, contrasted with 22
squares November-December 1932, the previous active area. Note *inactivity* January-February 1933 - 6 squares, February-March-7 squares, March-
April-6 squares. Up to 64, down to first 55 - first fair reaction in
bull move - main uptrend line is intact. At first 64 this line is actually broken. It is a tentative signal for a possible new deal in the
stock.

Up to this point no tips have been needed. We were weeks ahead in
March and April, 18-27 zone, and our one points kept us long to within
the 60-64 zone, in harmony with the main uptrend line. Now, we examine
the three point chart for confirmatory indications and check up on current position.

Our three point chart confirms each and every indication. We believe it speaks for itself, and does so eloquently. A clear downtrend
was established by AA, with confirmed culmination in the 18-22 zone, a
flat bottom, and another semi-catapult at 27. The confirmatory catapult
at 37 is distinct. DD line warned us to stay long, - note satisfactory
rising angle,-and then - the sharp run up beyond the consolidation area,
36-42 to 64. The decline, 64-49 is, of course, a major correction, the
first of its kind since April, when the stock turned at 18.

The old practical *base*, from former run up 19-38, was decided by
strong resistance at 35 on three point chart. There were three 35s,
five 36s, six 37s, indicating increasing support. Attempts to depress
the stock obviously met stout resistance. From 35 to 64 is 29 points.
A half-way reaction, traditional fifty per cent correction theory, called
for a 14-15 point decline. At this writing the low has been 49, 15
points from top at 64. There is no indication, as yet, that the decline has been checked nor that the major upswing is over. We must
now await the further development of our picture.

58

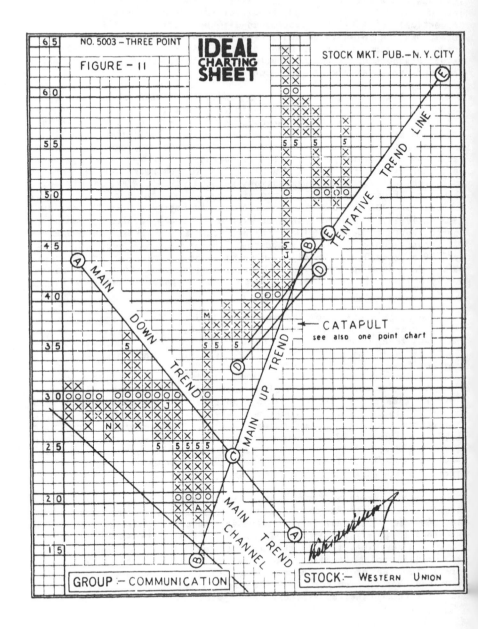

XVI.   ANTICIPATING MAJOR CYCLES BY MEANS OF THIS METHOD

Perfection is no more to be attained than infallibility.

When it is claimed that the Point and Figure Method has inherent possibilities of making or saving hundreds of points, the best evidence is here presented. That such a rise and fall took place within six months, that both major moves involving hundreds of points were completed, from base to peak and vice versa within a few weeks, is a remarkable example of the possibilities, for profit, through an intelligent understanding of the stock market.

We ask the student to realize that the possibilities are *there*, plainly apparent from the evidence. Whether or not we may succeed, in garnering the major profits appearing from such a future opportunity, is beside the point. It has been done - *by this Method*. It may be done again.

We will attempt to follow the market during its most hectic and, at times, most critical phases, the historical rise and fall of the latter half of 1929. Few such extreme examples in market history exist, considering time factor and distance travelled. It is a good testing ground for us. Let us travel through and over it, with the Point and Figure Method as our guide.

The N. Y. Times Averages, 50 stocks have been selected for illustration. Any other popular group such as the Herald-Tribune or the Dow-Jones would have answered the purpose. We have chosen the Times group because it happens to be a well known group to illustrate. This great daily has a worldwide circulation, and its averages are accessible to all.

The graphic record of these averages is drawn on a five point chart compiled from its one point moves figured daily. We strongly urge every reader to keep a five point record summation such as this, of any recognized group of averages. Its value will become apparent.

At the beginning of June 1929 the bull market of 1928-1929 was still sitting pretty with no visible evidence of major reversal in sight. The averages stood at 235 with indications ranging from neutral to trend up. We might have anticipated a change of front below 230. At 238 the averages not only were on the catapult, but registered a strong reversal from previous shakeout 237-231. We hardly needed our one points prior to 238 to realize that a 7 point advance in averages was a strongly bullish indication. The next vertical climb to 248 justified a correction. It came with a 6 point decline less than half way, then a further 14 point rise to 256, followed by a 5 point minor reaction. Here was a critical position, below 250. However, the averages held the line.

An ideally bullish pattern was beginning to form 250-253, with the averages on another catapult at 257, and a strong technical position proven by a straight 18 *point advance* to 269, the strongest rally yet, contrasted with 17 points and 14 points previously. This major rise partly fulfilled the anticipations of the professionals, who had looked for the spectacular run-in of shorts which duly occurred in the 250-255 zone.   This major demonstration was better than its predecessors, and a real advertisement for the market. This and its successor was it.

The long legs that formed here are typical of major operations, or manipulation if you care to call it that. Called also, facetiously, the push up because of its vigorous and daring characteristics, it is typical, and favored by the powerful professional element. The push up is clearly indicated at this point.

A minor reaction followed this major advance, 5 points exactly, a mere nominal correction. Then follows a 16 point major advance into new high ground at 280 from the last catapult formation at 270. The 280 line marked the first real battle ground of the bulls and bears, where the latter brought their heavy artillery to weaken the victorious, aggressive June--July 1929 bull campaign, hitherto without a setback.

Attention is called to the well-defined character of the picture so far - as shown by the five point moves only.   It is not so clear by any other Method.   Where is the investor or trader, worthy of the name, who would have used this Method and then hesitated being long and staying long from 230 to 280, with never a sign or cloud of danger? There are no such signs here as yet. On the contrary, there are many potential indications of higher prices.

Up to now we have no main trend line except theoretically with mental or actual stops moved up from 230, 240, 250, 260, 273, etc. There was no need to be particular about a few points!

We are compelled to await a major reversal, a real reaction before plotting a trend direction line, such as we made subsequently.   So far, we have only had technical readjustments, normal 5 and 6 point corrections, but no indication whatever of a major reversal. Up to 280 the Method says, stay long and await further indications.

A trading area begins to form at 275-280, with minor moves averaging 5-6 points, then a new high move 285, a 5 point correction, a 5 point rise to double top, a 6 point decline, a 6 point advance to treble top; a 7 point decline - a cautionary signal - than a 5 point rise to 283. Here the Method points to the balancing of forces - bulls and bears - supply and demand - and the great advance to date.   A fair correction must be expected.   This is the first real major trading area, a real congestion zone.   What is going to happen?

Let us reason it out. we must let the market dictate its own course. The former catapult level was 270.   That was where this operation began. We have already had a 55 point rise from 230.   A half way reaction would be down to 258 - too much to expect as yet! Let us allow a maximum of one third down as an ample major reaction, with a decision and reservation If the market should do this with an 18 point reaction down to around 265 we get out on the next advance or move up our stops.   What happens? A decline to 274 only is followed by a major rise of 14 points to 288, showing the market is well in hand and that the right people have the stocks as yet.   This is subsequently confirmed.   A 16 point decline follows to 272. With a quick face-about for 13 points, considered a strong rally indeed, the obstinate 285 mark is reached for the sixth time.

The Method says: *spectacular things must happen if the 285 re-sistance is overcome.*   It calls attention also to the possible danger suggested by the air-pocket formation under 280, *a perfect arched ellipse,* nearly always a sign of *potential* danger. However, the averages have be-haved bullishly, declining far less than a third, with an excellent new base around 275 and *now -- a clearly defined main trend line.*

From here on, we play safe and determine to stop everything men-tally, if not actually, at 270 because of clear evidence of major support there, the market's ability to rebound from there, and proof that campaign headquarters are just below 275. The last lines of defense, all the am-munition, all the money, all the hopes of the bulls are around 270.

The next major rally to 294 - a typical 13 point move - is accom-plished without much ado, a normal 6 point reaction, a 7 point rise to a new high at 295, a typical 5 point reaction, and then - the big push for-ward and upward, to be expected from the preceding tactics, to 302. *The Method's anticipation of what would happen about 295 was correct!* To have awaited a new catapult formation at 289, was again very profitable, new *very* high ground it is true, but - who knew? The sharp upward angle formed by the union of lines at the last 282, the last 291, upward inter-mediate trend line, with solid support in the 290-295 zone is also indi-cative of interesting action to come.

Conventional movements follow 302 with slight rallies and declines, and new highs, at 307 and then 308.   A long line begins forming at 300, indicating *major* distribution or accumulation. Which? Reference to our one point chart for a closer analysis of the work at 300 is desirable. It is not reproduced here for lack of space.`   This reveals that it is *one of the longest lines* at the average highest point yet! The Method says, *Look out.* Our real salvation is either to (a) place a stop under the main trend line already made, or (b) permit the market just *one* good reaction and/or sell on rally, or move up stops.

Now follows a reaction of 11 points to 297, a normal 6 point rally to 303, then a sharp 10 point reaction to 293. This is not so reassuring. The picture is getting dangerous. We have an airpocket under 300 - an-other arched ellipse.   Additionally, the cycle from 275 our practical base to 305 the practical peak *is showing signs of great fatigue.*

We are here permitted to call attention to the permissability of noting fundamentals at times. With new, all-time highs established, fur-ious trading for months, stocks quoted at 20 to 30 times earning power, Federal Reserve Bank warnings, The Secretary of the Treasury recommending the public to buy bonds, and the perfectly *obvious* need for great cau-tion, the Method becomes more insistent, more valuable. It warns that stops be placed below the main trend lines, not only of averages but of all individual stocks.

The decline to 293, a real correction from 308, *is on the main trend line,* and is almost a conventional half way reaction from the last 272 base to the new 308 peak.   The latter semi-cycle traveled 36 points up, and half way back would be down to 290.   Therefore, this major de-cline acted according to tradition with a 3 point margin of safety to spare!

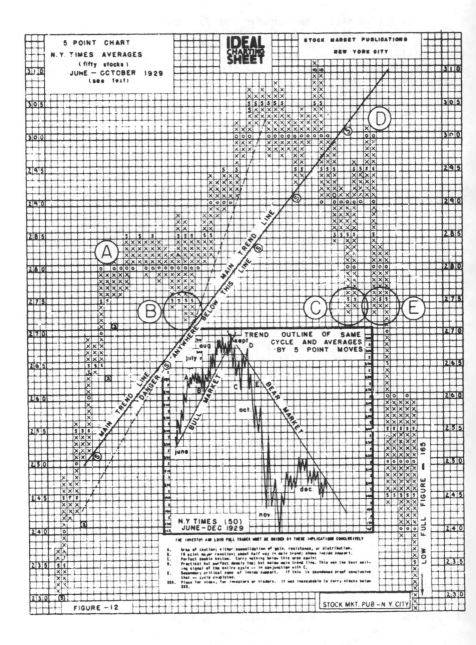

FIGURE — 12

The Method now says; *hold the line on the bull side, follow up any further major advances with stops.*

The averages then rebounded from the main trend line, and a new all-time high was made at 311. This was accomplished by a conventional II point rise from 293 to 304, a 5 point normal decline to 299, and then - the grand climax; the final I2 point quick advance to the top, at 311.

We have guided you over this great major operation in great detail in order to show you not only the working of our mind, but *just how the Method reasons it out,* and just why the five point major move chart, compiled from one points, is absolutely essential.

What followed is rather clear. Once the main trend line was abandoned on the upside, the entire picture was altered with dramatic suddenness.

There never was an excuse for anybody to carry stocks below this line after 311 was reached. The line of demarcation between safety and danger became absolutely clear. With five points, such as these, the Method never compromised. It had then, and has now - no ifs or buts. From 251 in June to 272 in August thence to 293 in September and beyond, is but the same *as charting a course by airline* across this continent or the Atlantic.

When supply overcame demand below the 300 level and the main trend line, the major bullish constructive powers obviously changed their tactics. That stocks were allowed to find a natural level, at the old support lines B and C around the critical 275 point was a clear confession from the first rebound at that point, and the double bottom there that the bag was being held by those interests right there.

The subsequent spectacular advance from 273 to 296, and final but feeble incomplete double top at 301 was evidence of frantic attempts to liquidate support stock acquired in the 275 headquarters' zone. This major recoil, a maximum of 28 points, failed to *reach or touch* the main trend line on the bullish side.

The Method said here: *go short with a stop at 305.* That was the point where a continuation of the rally would have crossed the bullish side of the main trend line.

From this point the great 1929 decline was on, in full force and fury. The old supporting lines at 275 were reached for the third and last time making a perfect triple bottom. It was extremely profitable to go short, at the market, or on rallies, even from 275, after the major decline of 36 points in *the averages.*

The market thereafter did not halt its downward plunge till 165 was reached!

The entire bull cycle was undoubtedly completed when 275 was reached for the third and last time. Reference to the key chart of the entire cycle will show tnat to have sold out and gone short even there, at 275, meant safety and profit within the *major upper strata* of a tremendous rise, and prior to a tremendous fall.

....

CONCLUSION

The public ought to know how! The panic and disaster of 1929-1933 would have been prevented had more people known "what it was all about." The peaks and valleys of booms and depressions *can* be and *should* be moderated by general dissemination of information and education. If enough buyers can be educated and found when prices are *reasonable* and the technical condition is *right*, their mass power is an economic help and a stabilizer.

If a sufficient number of investors and traders, recognizing a weak technical condition and an exaggerated price, can be induced to stay out of the market, it would be "Love's labor lost" for the professional operators and their subordinates to attempt to unload stocks on those who have been forewarned by study.

We are submitting the Point and Figure Method for your edification and enlightenment, after twenty years study of market movements and allied subjects. Let not the modest format of this work nor its low price serve as a yardstick of its immediate or future value to you. You will soon find yourself thinking in terms of Points and Figures, from which time on in our opinion, your investing and trading will be more successful.

The thoughts and/or angles of reasoning may strike familiar chords to old-timers in the Street. The interpretations, diagnosis and conclusions are the result of our own research. Many bright minds and able commentators have contributed liberally to the sum total of what we call "Market Knowledge" in the financial field.* They also deserve the thanks of the public and we are indebted to them.

Inasmuch as the progress of the student may be slow at first in assimilating the principles that are the warp and woof of this basic Method, discouragement should not be felt if occasionally his conclusions seem to be contradicted in the early stages by market action.

Test and re-test your reasoning and conclusions. Money need not be involved in investing or trading by this Method. Theoretical trades will be cheaper and more interesting until knowledge, familarity and confidence is acquired.

After such acquisition test this Method with actual trades, in uniform lots. Divide your contemplated transaction into four or five equal lots. Practice diversification. Place the eggs into many different baskets. Trust a logical, proven Method such as this, to give the results you seek. *It can and will come!* Keep at it until proficiency is attained.

It will be a pleasure for the author to help his readers, wherever and whenever it is felt that help is needed, in order to explain difficult points, or to place a longer experience behind any particular implication, interpretation or conclusion. Consider the author entirely at your service, without obligation on your part.

*My particular thanks are due Mr. Owen Taylor, my colleague, for his untiring assistance and valued suggestions.